OSBORNE REVISE!

ACCA

ACCA F7 Financial Reporting

NOTES

Published by Osborne Books Limited
Unit 2
The Business Centre
Molly Millars Lane
Wokingham
Berkshire RG41 2QZ

Tel 01905 748071

Email books@osbornebooks.co.uk

Website www.osbornebooks.co.uk

Printed and bound in Great Britain.

British Library Cataloguing in Publication Data

A catalogue record for this book is available from the British Library

ISBN: 978-1-911198-28-4

Acknowledgements

This Product includes propriety content of the International Accounting Standards Board which is overseen by the IFRS Foundation, and is used with the express permission of the IFRS Foundation under licence. All rights reserved. No part of this publication may be reproduced, stored in a retrieval system, or transmitted in any form or by any means, electronic, mechanical, photocopying, recording, or otherwise, without prior written permission of Kaplan Publishing and the IFRS Foundation.

The IFRS Foundation logo, the IASB logo, the IFRS for SMEs logo, the "Hexagon Device", "IFRS Foundation", "eIFRS", "IAS", "IASB", "IFRS for SMEs", "IFRS", "IASs", "IFRSs", "International Accounting Standards" and "International Financial Reporting Standards", "IFRIC" and "IFRS Taxonomy" are **Trade Marks** of the IFRS Foundation.

Trade Marks

The IFRS Foundation logo, the IASB logo, the IFRS for SMEs logo, the "Hexagon Device", "IFRS Foundation", "eIFRS", "IAS", "IASB", "IFRS for SMEs", "NIIF" IASs" "IFRS", "IFRSs", "International Accounting Standards", "International Financial Reporting Standards", "IFRIC", "SIC" and "IFRS Taxonomy".

Further details of the Trade Marks including details of countries where the Trade Marks are registered or applied for are available from the Foundation on request.

This product contains material that is ©Financial Reporting Council Ltd (FRC). Adapted and reproduced with the kind permission of the Financial Reporting Council. All rights reserved. For further information, please visit www.frc.org.uk or call +44 (0)20 7492 2300.

CONTENTS

Chapter		Page

This document references IFRS® Standards and IAS® Standards, which are authored by the International Accounting Standards Board (the Board), and published in the 2016 IFRS Standards Red Book.

HOW TO USE THESE *ACCA Notes*

These *ACCA Notes* have been designed to help you to:

- **Renew** your approach to syllabus areas that might not have been clear first time around. Use them to supplement your learning and to help you to clarify details of the syllabus of which you are unsure. It is easy to look things up using the detailed index and contents page and find quickly the topic you need help with

- **Refresh** topics you have covered before but may have forgotten. If it is a while since you studied a topic which underpins a higher level subject that you now need to study, for example, use them as a refresher tool to remind yourself of what you have already learnt

- **Revise** and make the best use of your time before your examinations. Take advantage of the summarised topics, learning summaries, summary diagrams, key points, definitions and exam tips to support your revision in the critical period leading up to your real exam.

PREPARING FOR THE EXAM

To pass your exam you need an understanding of the syllabus and exam technique is vital. These *ACCA Notes* follow the syllabus with succinct coverage, offering tips on how to get the best results in the exam.

ACCA Notes – ICONS

LEARNING SUMMARY

The 'learning summary' provides details of the key learning objectives of each section of content.

DEFINITION

The 'definition' boxes highlight and explain key terms.

KEY POINT

The 'key point' boxes emphasise key points which are fundamental to your understanding of the syllabus.

Do you understand?

The 'do you understand' boxes contain short form questions which are not necessarily exam style, but which test that you have understood the core syllabus content before you progress onto exam style questions.

PAPER INFORMATION

The aim of ACCA Paper F7, Financial Reporting, is to develop knowledge and skills in understanding and applying accounting standards and the theoretical framework in the preparation of financial statements of entities, including groups and how to analyse and interpret those financial statements.

SYLLABUS

A   **A CONCEPTUAL FRAMEWORK FOR FINANCIAL REPORTING**

1   **The need for a conceptual framework**

(a)   Describe what is meant by a conceptual framework for financial reporting. [2] **Ch. 6**

(b)   Discuss whether a conceptual framework is necessary and what an alternative system might be. [2] **Ch. 6**

(c)   Discuss what is meant by relevance and faithful representation and describe the qualities that enhance these characteristics. [2] **Ch. 6**

(d)   Discuss whether faithful representation constitutes more than compliance with accounting standards. [1] **Ch. 6**

(e)   Discuss what is meant by understandability and verifiability in relation to the provision of financial information. [2] **Ch. 6**

(f)   Discuss the importance of comparability and timeliness to users of financial statements. [2] **Ch. 6**

(g)   Discuss the principle of comparability in accounting for changes in accounting policies. [2] **Ch. 8**

2   **Recognition and measurement**

(a)   Define what is meant by 'recognition' in financial statements and discuss the recognition criteria. [2] **Ch. 6**

(b)   Apply the recognition criteria to: [2] **Ch. 6**

  (i)   assets and liabilities

  (ii)   income and expenses.

(c)   Explain and compute amounts using the following measures: [2] **Ch. 7**

  (i)   historical cost

  (ii)   current cost

  (iii)   net realisable value

  (iv)   present value of future cash flows.

  (v)   fair value

(d)   Discuss the advantages and disadvantages of historical cost accounting. [2] **Ch. 7**

(e)   Discuss whether the use of current value accounting overcomes the problems of historical cost accounting. [2] **Ch. 7**

(f)   Describe the concept of financial and physical capital maintenance and how this affects the determination of profits. [1] **Ch. 7**

3   **Regulatory framework**

(a)   Explain why a regulatory framework is needed, including the advantages and disadvantages of IFRS over a national regulatory framework. [2] **Ch. 6**

(b) Explain why accounting standards on their own are not a complete regulatory framework. [2] **Ch. 6**

(c) Distinguish between a principles based and a rules based framework and discuss whether they can be complementary. [1] **Ch. 6**

(d) Describe the IASB's standard setting process including revisions to and interpretations of standards. [2] **Ch. 6**

(e) Explain the relationship of national standard setters to the IASB in respect of the standard setting process. [2] **Ch. 6**

4   The concepts and principles of groups and consolidated financial statements

(a) Describe the concept of a group as a single economic unit. [2] **Ch.16**

(b) Explain and apply the definition of a subsidiary within relevant accounting standards. [2] **Ch.16**

(c) Using accounting standards and other regulation, identify and outline the circumstances in which a group is required to prepare consolidated financial statements. [2] **Ch.16**

(d) Describe the circumstances when a group may claim exemption from the preparation of consolidated financial statements. [2] **Ch.16**

(e) Explain why directors may not wish to consolidate a subsidiary and when this is permitted by accounting standards and other applicable regulation. [2] **Ch.16**

(f) Explain the need for using coterminous year ends and uniform accounting policies when preparing consolidated financial statements. [2] **Ch.16**

(g) Explain why it is necessary to eliminate intra group transactions. [2] **Ch.16**

(h) Explain the objective of consolidated financial statements. [2] **Ch.16**

(i) Explain why it is necessary to use fair values for the consideration for an investment in a subsidiary together with the fair values of a subsidiary's identifiable assets and liabilities when preparing consolidated financial statements. [2] **Ch.17**

(j) Define an associate and explain the principles and reasoning for the use of equity accounting. [2] **Ch.19**

B   ACCOUNTING FOR TRANSACTIONS IN FINANCIAL STATEMENTS

1   Tangible non-current assets

(a) Define and compute the initial measurement of a non-current asset (including borrowing costs and an asset that has been self-constructed). [2] **Ch. 2**

(b) Identify subsequent expenditure that may be capitalised, distinguishing between capital and revenue items. [2] **Ch. 2**

(c) Discuss the requirements of relevant accounting standards in relation to the revaluation of non-current assets. [2] **Ch. 2**

(d) Account for revaluation and disposal gains and losses for non-current assets. [2] **Ch. 2**

(e) Compute depreciation based on the cost and revaluation models and on assets that have two or more significant parts (complex assets). [2] **Ch. 2**

(f) Discuss why the treatment of investment properties should differ from other properties. [2] **Ch. 2**

(g) Apply the requirements of relevant accounting standards to an investment property. [2] **Ch. 2**

2   Intangible assets

(a)   Discuss the nature and accounting treatment of internally generated and purchased intangibles. [2] **Ch. 3**

(b)   Distinguish between goodwill and other intangible assets. [2] **Ch. 3**

(c)   Describe the criteria for the initial recognition and measurement of intangible assets. [2] **Ch. 3**

(d)   Describe the subsequent accounting treatment, including the principle of impairment tests in relation to goodwill. [2] **Ch. 3 & Ch. 17**

(e)   Indicate why the value of purchase consideration for an investment may be less than the value of the acquired identifiable net assets and how the difference should be accounted for. [2] **Ch. 17**

(f)   Describe and apply the requirements of relevant accounting standards to research and development expenditure. [2] **Ch. 3**

3   Impairment of assets

(a)   Define, calculate and account for an impairment loss. [2] **Ch. 4**

(b)   Account for the reversal of an impairment loss on an individual asset. [2] **Ch. 4**

(c)   Identify the circumstances that may indicate impairments to assets. [2] **Ch. 4**

(d)   Describe what is meant by a cash generating unit. [2] **Ch. 4**

(e)   State the basis on which impairment losses should be allocated, and allocate an impairment loss to the assets of a cash generating unit. [2] **Ch. 4**

4   Inventory and biological assets

(a)   Describe and apply the principles of inventory valuation. [2] **Ch. 8**

(b)   Apply the requirements of relevant accounting standards for biological assets. [2] **Ch. 8**

5   Financial instruments

(a)   Explain the need for an accounting standard on financial instruments. [1] **Ch. 10**

(b)   Define financial instruments in terms of financial assets and financial liabilities. [1] **Ch. 10**

(c)   Explain and account for the factoring of receivables. [1] **Ch. 10**

(d)   Indicate for the following categories of financial instruments how they should be measured and how any gains and losses from subsequent measurement should be treated in the financial statements: [1] **Ch. 10**

    (i)   amortised cost

    (ii)   fair value through other comprehensive income (including where an irrevocable election has been made for equity investments that are not held for trading).

    (iii)   fair value through profit or loss

(e)   Distinguish between debt and equity capital. [2] **Ch. 10**

(f)   Apply the requirements of relevant accounting standards to the issue and finance costs of: [2] **Ch. 10**

    (i)   equity

    (ii)   redeemable preference shares and debt instruments with no conversion rights (principle of amortised cost).

    (iii)   convertible debt

6   Leasing

(a)   Account for right-of-use assets and lease liabilities in the records of the lessee. [2] **Ch. 9**

(b)   Explain the exemption from the recognition criteria for leases in the records of the lessee. [2] **Ch. 9**

(c)   Account for sale and leaseback agreements. [2] **Ch. 9**

7   Provisions and events after the reporting period

(a)   Explain why an accounting standard on provisions is necessary. [2] **Ch.15**

(b)   Distinguish between legal and constructive obligations. [2] **Ch. 15**

(c)   State when provisions may and may not be made and demonstrate how they should be accounted for. [2] **Ch. 15**

(d)   Explain how provisions should be measured. [1] Ch. 15

(e)   Define contingent assets and liabilities and describe their accounting treatment and required disclosures. [2] **Ch. 15**

(f)   Identify and account for: [2] **Ch. 15**

    (i)   warranties/guarantees

    (ii)   onerous contracts

    (iii)   environmental and similar provisions

    (iv)   provisions for future repairs or refurbishments

(g)   Events after the reporting period:

    (i)   distinguish between and account for adjusting and non-adjusting events after the reporting period. [2] **Ch. 15**

    (ii)   identify items requiring separate disclosure, including their accounting treatment and required disclosures. [2] **Ch. 15**

8   Taxation

(a)   Account for current taxation in accordance with relevant accounting standards. [2] **Ch. 13**

(b)   Explain the effect of taxable temporary differences on accounting and taxable profits. [2] **Ch. 13**

(c)   Compute and record deferred tax amounts in the financial statements. [2] **Ch. 13**

9   Reporting financial performance

(a)   Discuss the importance of identifying and reporting the results of discontinued operations. [2] **Ch. 5**

(b)   Define and account for non-current assets held for sale and discontinued operations. [2] **Ch. 5**

(c)   Indicate the circumstances where separate disclosure of material items of income and expense is required. [2] **Ch. 1 & Ch. 5**

(d)   Account for changes in accounting estimates, changes in accounting policy and correction of prior period errors. [2] **Ch. 8**

(e)   Earnings per share (EPS)

    (i)   calculate the EPS in accordance with relevant accounting standards (dealing with bonus issues, full market value issues and rights issues). [2] **Ch. 14**

    (ii)   explain the relevance of the diluted EPS and calculate the diluted EPS involving convertible debt and share options (warrants). [2] **Ch. 14**

10 Revenue

(a) Explain and apply the principles of recognition of revenue: [2] **Ch. 12**

  (i) identification of contracts

  (ii) identification of performance obligations

  (iii) determination of transaction price

  (iv) allocation of the price to performance obligations

  (v) recognition of revenue when/as performance obligations are satisfied

(b) Explain and apply the criteria for recognising revenue generated from contracts where performance obligations are satisfied over time or at a point in time. [2] **Ch. 12**

(c) Describe the acceptable methods for measuring progress towards complete satisfaction of a performance obligation. [2] **Ch. 12**

(d) Explain and apply the criteria for the recognition of contract costs. [2] **Ch. 12**

(e) Apply the principles of recognition of revenue, and specifically account for the following types of transaction: [2] **Ch. 12**

  (i) principal versus agent

  (ii) repurchase agreements

  (iii) bill and hold arrangements

  (iv) consignments

(f) Prepare financial statement extracts for contracts where performance obligations are satisfied over time. [2] **Ch. 12**

11 Government grants

(a) Apply the provisions of relevant accounting standards in relation to accounting for government grants. [2] **Ch. 2**

12 Foreign currency transactions

(a) Explain the difference between functional and presentation currency and explain why adjustments for foreign currency transactions are necessary. [2] **Ch. 11**

(b) Account for the translation of foreign currency transactions and monetary/non-monetary foreign currency items at the reporting date. [2] **Ch. 11**

C ANALYSING AND INTERPRETING THE FINANCIAL STATEMENTS OF SINGLE ENTITIES AND GROUPS

1 Limitations of financial statements

(a) Indicate the problems of using historic information to predict future performance and trends. [2] **Ch. 21**

(b) Discuss how financial statements may be manipulated to produce a desired effect (creative accounting, window dressing). [2] **Ch. 21**

(c) Explain why figures in a statement of financial position may not be representative of average values throughout the period for example, due to: [2] **Ch. 21**

  (i) seasonal trading

  (ii) major asset acquisitions near the end of the accounting period.

(d) Explain how the use of consolidated financial statements might limit interpretation techniques. [2] **Ch. 21**

2 **Calculation and interpretation of accounting ratios and trends to address users' and stakeholders' needs**

(a) Define and compute relevant financial ratios. [2] **Ch. 21**

(b) Explain what aspects of performance specific ratios are intended to assess. [2] **Ch. 21**

(c) Analyse and interpret ratios to give an assessment of an entity's/group's performance and financial position in comparison with: [2] **Ch. 21**

    (i) previous period's financial statements

    (ii) another similar entity/group for the same reporting period

    (iii) industry average ratios.

(d) Interpret an entity's financial statements to give advice from the perspectives of different stakeholders. [2] **Ch. 21**

(e) Discuss how the interpretation of current value based financial statements would differ from those using historical cost based accounts. [1] **Ch. 21**

3 **Limitations of interpretation techniques**

(a) Discuss the limitations in the use of ratio analysis for assessing corporate performance. [2] **Ch. 21**

(b) Discuss the effect that changes in accounting policies or the use of different accounting policies between entities can have on the ability to interpret performance. [2] **Ch. 21**

(c) Indicate other information, including non-financial information, that may be of relevance to the assessment of an entity's performance. [2] **Ch. 21**

(d) Compare the usefulness of cash flow information with that of a statement of profit or loss or a statement of profit or loss and other comprehensive income. [2] **Ch. 22**

(e) Interpret a statement of cash flows (together with other financial information) to assess the performance and financial position of an entity. [2] **Ch. 22**

(i) explain why the trend of EPS may be a more accurate indicator of performance than a company's profit trend and the importance of EPS as a stock market indicator. [2] **Ch. 14**

(ii) discuss the limitations of using EPS as a performance measure. [2] **Ch. 14**

4 **Specialised, not-for-profit and public sector entities**

(a) Explain how the interpretation of the financial statement of a specialised, not-for-profit or public sector organisation might differ from that of a profit making entity by reference to the different aims, objectives and reporting requirements. [1] **Chs. 6 & 21**

D **PREPARATION OF FINANCIAL STATEMENTS**

1 **Preparation of single entity financial statements**

(a) Prepare an entity's statement of financial position and statement of profit or loss and other comprehensive income in accordance with the structure and content prescribed within IFRS and with accounting treatments as identified within syllabus areas A, B and C. [2] **Ch. 1**

(b) Prepare and explain the contents and purpose of the statement of changes in equity. [2] **Ch. 1**

(c) Prepare a statement of cash flows for a single entity (not a group) in accordance with relevant accounting standards using the direct and the indirect method. [2] **Ch. 22**

2   Preparation of consolidated financial statements including an associate

(a)   Prepare a consolidated statement of financial position for a simple group (parent and one subsidiary and associate) dealing with pre- and post-acquisition profits, non-controlling interests and consolidated goodwill. [2] **Chs. 17 & 19**

(b)   Prepare a consolidated statement of profit or loss and consolidated statement of profit or loss and other comprehensive income for a simple group dealing with an acquisition in the period and non-controlling interest. [2] **Ch. 18**

(c)   Explain and account for other reserves (e.g. share premium and revaluation reserves). [1] **Ch. 17**

(d)   Account for the effects in the financial statements of intra-group trading. [2] **Chs. 17 & 19**

(e)   Account for the effects of fair value adjustments (including their effect on consolidated goodwill) to: [2] **Chs. 17 & 18**

(i)   depreciating and non-depreciating non-current assets

(ii)   inventory

(iii) monetary liabilities

(iv) assets and liabilities not included in the subsidiary's own statement of financial position, including contingent assets and liabilities

(f)   Account for goodwill impairment. [2] **Chs. 17 & 18**

(g)   Describe and apply the required accounting treatment of consolidated goodwill. [2] **Chs. 17 & 18**

(h)   Explain and illustrate the effect of a disposal of a parent's investment in a subsidiary in the parent's individual financial statements and/or those of the group (restricted to disposals of the parent's entire investment in the subsidiary). [2] **Ch. 20**

The numbers in square brackets indicate the intellectual depth at which the subject area could be assessed within the examination. Level 1 (knowledge and comprehension) broadly equates with the Knowledge module, Level 2 (application and analysis) with the Skills module and Level 3 (synthesis and evaluation) to the Professional level. However, lower level skills can continue to be assessed as you progress through each module and level.

TOP 10 TIPS TO IMPROVE YOUR RESULT

Be organised and plan your study time – there are more tips on how to do this below.

'Mens sana in corpore sano' – prepare your body; sleep well and eat right as a healthy body leads to a healthy mind!

Study according to your learning style – different people have different learning styles. Some people are visual learners, some people prefer sound, some need physical motion – try out different methods to see what works best for you.

Try using a study buddy – this could be someone taking the same exam, or a friend or family member.

Revise knowledge efficiently – stay focused, stop procrastinating and don't let your mind wander.

Read questions very carefully – many students fail to answer the actual question set. Read the question once right through and then again more slowly. Make note of key words in the question when you read through it.

Ensure you know the structure of the exam – how many questions (and of what type) you will be expected to answer. During your revision, attempt all the different styles of questions you may be asked.

Be a good test-taker. Get lots of practice – the ACCA release sample assessments and practice CBE mock exams are available.

Read good newspapers and professional journals, especially ACCA's *Student Accountant* – this can give you a distinct advantage in the exam.

Adopt a positive mental attitude. You may have nerves and feel anxious but with the correct preparation and practice you can have confidence in your ability to succeed.

PLAN YOUR STUDY TIME

Decide which times of the week you will devote to revising.

Put the times you plan to revise onto a study plan for the weeks from now until the exam and set yourself targets for each period of revision, ensuring that you cover the whole syllabus.

If you are studying for more than one paper at a time, try to mix and match your subjects as this can help you to keep motivated and see each subject in its broader context.

When working through your course, compare your progress with your plan and, if you fall behind, re-plan your work (perhaps including extra sessions). If you are ahead, do some extra revision/practice questions.

EXTRA QUESTIONS

Practising exam standard questions is a critical part of your revision.

Specimen Exams and Practice Tests are available from
http://www.accaglobal.com/gb/en/student/exam-support-resources.html

and Exam Kits and Mock Exams in the style of the real exam can be obtained from

http://kaplan-publishing.kaplan.co.uk/acca-books/pages/acca-books.aspx.

1 Introduction to published accounts

The following topics are covered in this chapter:

- Preparation of financial statements for companies
- Format of financial statements
- Profit-orientated and public sector entities

1.1 PREPARATION OF FINANCIAL STATEMENTS FOR COMPANIES

LEARNING SUMMARY

After studying this section you should be able to:

- understand what comprises a set of financial statements.

The statement of financial position

This statement summarises the assets, liabilities and equity balances of the business at the end of the reporting period.

The statement of profit or loss and other comprehensive income

This statement summarises the revenues earned and expenses incurred by the business throughout the reporting period.

The statement of changes in equity

This statement summarises the movement in equity balances i.e. share capital, share premium, revaluation surplus and retained earnings.

The statement of cash flows

This statement summarises the cash paid and received throughout the reporting period.

The notes to the financial statements

The notes to the financial statements comprise a statement of accounting policies and any other disclosures required to enable to the shareholders and other users of the financial statements to make informed judgements about the business.

1.2 FORMAT OF FINANCIAL STATEMENTS

LEARNING SUMMARY

After studying this section you should be able to:

- outline the statement of financial position
- outline the statement of profit or loss and other comprehensive income
- outline the statement of changes in equity

KEY POINT The required formats for published company financial statements are provided by IAS 1 Presentation of Financial Statements.

The statement of financial position

Statement of financial position for *(name of business)* as at *(date of period end)*		
	$	$
Non-current assets		
Property, plant and equipment	X	
Investments	X	
Intangibles	X	
		X
Current assets		
Inventories	X	
Trade and other receivables	X	
Prepayments	X	
Cash	X	
		X
Total assets		X
Equity		
Ordinary share capital	X	
Irredeemable preference share capital	X	
Share premium	X	
Reserves:		
Retained earnings	X	
		X
Non-current liabilities		
Loan notes		X
Current liabilities		
Trade and other payables X	X	
Overdrafts X	X	
Tax payable	X	
		X
Total equity and liabilities		X

The statement of profit or loss and other comprehensive income

Statement of profit or loss for *(name of business)* for the period ended *(date of period end)*	
	$
Revenue	X
Cost of sales	(X)
Gross profit	**X**
Distribution costs	(X)
Administrative expenses	(X)
Profit from operations	**X**
Investment income	X
Finance costs	(X)
Profit before tax	**X**
Tax expense	(X)
Net profit for the period	**X**
Other comprehensive income	
Items that will not be reclassified to profit or loss in future periods:	
Gain/loss on property revaluation in the year	X/(X)
Total comprehensive income for the year	**X**

KEY POINT An entity can choose to present the above information in the form of two separate statements:

- the statement of profit or loss for the year, and

- the statement of other comprehensive income for the year.

> You need to learn these proforma layouts.

The statement of changes in equity

	Share capital	Share premium	Revaluation surplus	Retained earnings	Total
	$	$	$	$	$
Balance at the beginning of the financial period	X	X	X	X	X
Equity shares issued	X	X			X
Total comprehensive income			X	X	X
Transfer to retained earnings (see chapter 2)			(X)	X	X
Dividends				(X)	(X)
Balance at the end of the financial period	X	X	X	X	X

1.3 PROFIT-ORIENTATED AND PUBLIC SECTOR ENTITIES

LEARNING SUMMARY

After studying this section you should be able to:

- understand the differences between profit-orientated and public sector entities.

	Profit-orientated	Public sector
Financial aims	Shareholder wealth	Value for money
Accountability	Shareholders	Trustees/government/public
Sources of finance	Share capital/loan	Loan/donations/subsidies

Do you understand?

1   The statement of financial position summarises the asset, liability and equity balances (i.e. the financial position of the entity) at the end of the accounting period.

True or false?

2   Dividends paid will be deducted from what balance on the statement of changes in equity?

(i)   share capital

(ii)   share premium

(iii)   revaluation surplus

(iv)   retained earnings

3   The financial aim for a profit-orientated entity is value for money.

True or false?

3 False. The financial aim for a profit-orientated entity is shareholder wealth.
2 (iv) dividends paid are deducted from the retained earnings balance.
1 True.

1 You have been asked to help prepare the financial statements of Kendall Ltd for the year ended 30 June 20X1. The entity's trial balance as at 30 June 20X1 is shown below.

	Debit $000	Credit $000
Share capital		50,000
Share premium		25,000
Revaluation reserve at 1 July 20X0		10,000
Land & buildings – value/cost	120,000	
accumulated depreciation at 1 July 20X0		22,500
Plant and equipment – cost	32,000	
accumulated depreciation at 1 July 20X0		18,000
Trade and other receivables	20,280	
Trade and other payables		8,725
5% bank loan repayable 20X5		20,000
Cash and cash equivalents	2,213	
Retained earnings at 1 July 20X0		12,920
Sales		100,926
Purchases	67,231	
Distribution costs	8,326	
Administrative expenses	7,741	
Inventories at 1 July 20X0	7,280	
Dividends paid	3,000	

The following information is relevant to the preparation of the financial statements:

(i) The inventories at the close of business on 30 June 20X1 cost $9,420,000.

(ii) Depreciation is to be provided for the year to 30 June 20X1 as follows:

Buildings 4% per annum Straight line basis

This should all be charged to administrative expenses

Plant and equipment 20% per annum Reducing balance basis

This is to be apportioned as follows:

	%
Cost of sales	70
Distribution costs	20
Administrative expenses	10

Land, which is non-depreciable, is included in the trial balance at a value of $40,000,000. At 30 June 20X1, a surveyor valued it at $54,000,000. This revaluation is to be included in the financial statements for the year ended 30 June 20X1.

(iii) It has been decided to write off a debt of $540,000 which will be charged to administrative expenses.

(iv) Included within distribution costs is $2,120,000 relating to an advertising campaign that will commence on 1 January 20X1 and run to 31 December 20X1.

(v) Loan interest has not yet been accounted for.

(vi) The tax charge for the year has been calculated at $2,700,000.

Required:

Prepare the statement of profit or loss and other comprehensive income of Kendall Ltd for the year ended 30 June 20X1 and the statement of financial position as at 30 June 20X1.

2 Tangible non-current assets

The following topics are covered in this chapter:
- Recognition and initial measurement
- Depreciation
- Revaluations
- Disclosure of Government assistance
- IAS 23 *Borrowing costs*
- IAS 40 *Investment property*

2.1 RECOGNITION AND INITIAL MEASUREMENT

LEARNING SUMMARY

After studying this section you should be able to:

- explain when an asset should be recognised
- compute the initial measurement of non-current asset
- distinguish between capital and revenue expenditure.

Recognition

KEY POINT Property, plant and equipment should be recognised as an asset when there is a probable flow of economic benefit and a reliable measure of cost.

Initial measurement

Property, plant and equipment should be initially measured at cost.

KEY POINT Cost should include all directly attributable costs necessary to bring the asset into use.

Includes:	Excludes:
capital expenditure:	revenue expenditure:
purchase price	repairs
delivery costs	renewals
legal fees	repainting
subsequent expenditure which enhances the asset	administration
trials and tests	general overheads
	training costs
	waste

Capital expenditure

Acquisition of non-current assets acquired for use in the business, not for resale.

Expenditure on existing non-current assets aimed at increasing their earning capacity.

Revenue expenditure

Expenditure relevant to the running of the business i.e. administration costs.

Expenditure on current assets i.e. inventory.

Expenditure on maintaining the earning capacity of non-current assets e.g. repairs and renewals.

Subsequent expenditure

Subsequent expenditure should only be capitalised if it:

- enhances the asset's economic benefits
- relates to an overhaul or major safety inspection
- replaces a component of a complex asset

Any expenditure not capitalised would be charged as revenue to the statement of profit or loss.

2.2 DEPRECIATION

Cost	Amount capitalised.
Useful economic life	Period over which economic benefits are expected to be derived from the asset.
Residual value	Amount that the asset is expected to be sold for at the end of its useful economic life.

Methods of depreciation

Straight line method	Reducing balance method	Machine hours

KEY POINT Depreciation must be charged from the date the asset is available for use, i.e. it is capable of operating in the manner intended by management.

Changing estimates

The same rates and methods of depreciation should be applied consistently throughout the life of their business. However, if the estimates of useful life and/or residual value are believed to be inappropriate a change is permitted. A new depreciation charge of the asset based on the revised estimate of useful life or residual value is calculated.

2.3 REVALUATIONS

LEARNING SUMMARY

After studying this section you should be able to:

*   explain the requirements of IAS 16 in relation to the revaluation of non-current assets.

Choices

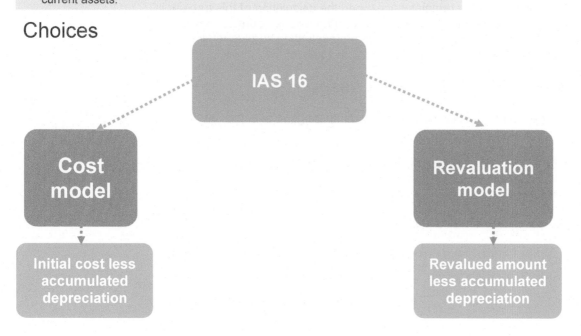

Accounting for revaluation

Dr	Accumulated depreciation account
Dr	Non-current asset cost account
Cr	Revaluation surplus (Other comprehensive income)

The accumulated depreciation is debited with the accumulated depreciation to date on the asset.

The non-current asset cost account is debited with the difference between the original cost and the revalued amount.

The revaluation surplus is credited with the difference between the carrying amount and the revalued amount.

Revaluation losses are charged as an expense to the statement of profit or loss.

Impact of revaluation

All assets in same class to be revalued	Revaluations must be kept up to date	Subsequent depreciation based on new value and remaining useful life

Annual reserves transfer

IAS 16 permits an annual transfer to be made from the revaluation surplus to retained earnings to offset the additional depreciation charged as a result of the revaluation. This transfer would be shown on the statement of changes in equity (see chapter 1).

Where the asset life remains unchanged the calculation of this transfer is simply the difference between the new and previous depreciation charge. If the asset life changes the transfer is the revaluation surplus relating to depreciated assets divided by the remaining asset life.

Disposal of a revalued asset

The gain on disposal is calculated by comparing the sale proceeds to the carrying amount.

KEY POINT There is an additional step required to clear any balance on the revaluation surplus in relation to the disposed asset.

The accounting entry for this is:

Dr	Revaluation surplus (Other comprehensive income)
Cr	Retained earnings (Other comprehensive income)

Contents of a non-current assets register:	
cost	location of asset
date of purchase	depreciation method
description of asset	expected useful life
serial/reference number	carrying amount

Do you understand?

1   A non-current asset was purchased by Bob on 1 January 20X1 for $48,000. It has an estimated useful economic life of 6 years and an estimated residual value of $8,500.

What would be the depreciation charge for this asset for the year ending 31 December 20X3 using straight line depreciation?

2   When a non-current asset has been revalued, the charge for depreciation should be based on the revalued amount and the remaining useful life of the asset.

True or false?

3   When an asset which has previously been revalued is disposed of, the corresponding amount in revaluation surplus remains there.

True or false?

3 False. It will be transferred from revaluation surplus to retained earnings.
2 True.
1 ($48,000 − $8,500)/6 = $6,583

2.4 DISCLOSURE OF GOVERNMENT ASSISTANCE

LEARNING SUMMARY

After studying this section you should be able to:

- apply the provisions of IAS 20 in relation to accounting for government grants.

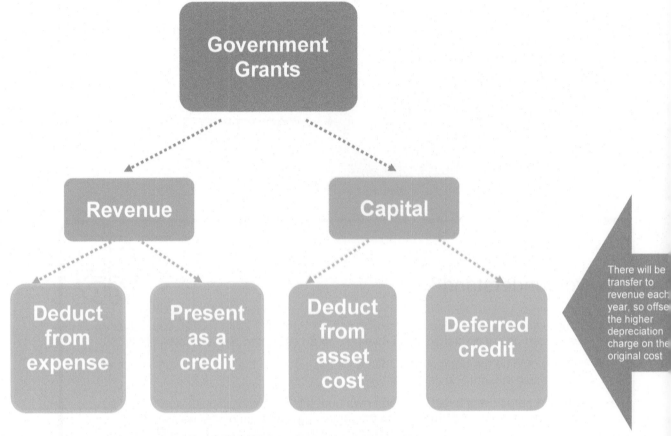

2.5 IAS 23 *BORROWING COSTS*

LEARNING SUMMARY

After studying this section you should be able to:

- explain the treatment of borrowing costs per IAS 23.

IAS 23 Treatment

KEY POINT Borrowing costs must be capitalised as part of the cost of an asset if that asset is a qualifying asset. A qualifying asset is one which necessarily takes a substantial time to get ready for is intended use or sale.

Commencement of capitalisation

Capitalisation commences when:

- expenditure for the asset is being incurred, and

- borrowing costs are being incurred, and

- activities that are necessary to prepare the asset for its intended use or sale are in progress.

Cessation of capitalisation

Capitalisation ceases when:

- substantially all the activities necessary to prepare the qualifying asset for its intended use or sale are complete, or

- there is an unplanned suspension of construction, e.g. due to industrial disputes.

Interest rate

The rate of interest to be used is:

- actual interest rate where specific funds borrowed, or

- weighted average of general borrowings where general borrowings used.

Weighted average calculation:

$$\frac{(\text{Loan 1} \times \%) + (\text{Loan 2} \times \%)}{\text{Total loan}}$$

2.6   IAS 40 *INVESTMENT PROPERTY*

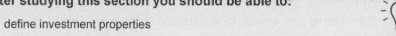

LEARNING SUMMARY

After studying this section you should be able to:

- define investment properties

- apply the requirements of IAS 40 for investment properties.

Investment property

DEFINITION Investment property is land and/or a building held for rental income and/or capital appreciation, rather than for use by the entity or for sale in the ordinary course of business.

Choices

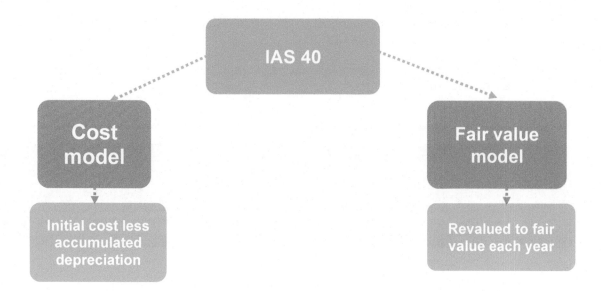

Cost model

KEY POINT The cost model for investment property is the same as for property held under IAS 16, with depreciation charged as an expense in the statement of profit or loss each year.

Fair value model

Investment property under the fair value model is accounted for differently to property under the IAS 16 revaluation model:

- investment property is revalued to fair value at the end of each year

- any gain or loss is taken to the statement of profit or loss, rather than other comprehensive income

- no depreciation is charged.

Transfers to and from investment property

KEY POINT If the fair value model for investment property is used, then the property should be revalued before being transferred between investment property and property, plant and equipment.

The way to remember this is that it's the final treatment under the old classification.

From investment property to property, plant and equipment:

- revalue using IAS 40 rules, taking gain or loss to profit or loss

From property, plant and equipment to investment property:

- revalue using IAS 16 rules taking gain or loss to revaluation surplus or profit or loss as appropriate

Do you understand?

1   A company can choose to capitalise borrowing costs as part of the cost of an asset if that asset is a qualifying asset.

   True or false?

2   Under the cost model for investment property there is no depreciation charge.

   True or false?

3   When a government grant for revenue expenditure is received it must be deducted from the expense it relates to.

   True or false?

1   False.   Borrowing costs must be capitalised if the asset is a qualifying asset.
2   False.   There is a depreciation charge to the statement of profit or loss each year.
3   False.   There is a choice between deducting it from the expense or presenting it as a credit on the statement of profit or loss.

1   **Which of the following items should be classified as capital expenditure?**

   A   Repairs to motor vans

   B   Depreciation of machinery

   C   Extension of premises

   D   Purchase of motor vans for resale

2   **Complete the sentence below by placing one of the following options into the space.**

   IAS 40 *Investment properties* defines an investment property as _____.

land or a buildings originally acquired to earn rentals, but maybe used by the entity in the ordinary course of business
land or a buildings held to earn rentals, or for capital appreciation or both, rather than for use in the entity or for sale by the entity in the ordinary course of business for a period of less than 12 months
land or a buildings held to earn rentals, or for capital appreciation or both, rather than for use in the entity or for sale by the entity in the ordinary course of business

3   **According to IAS 20 *Accounting for Government Grants and Disclosure of Government Assistance*, which TWO of the following statements explain how a capital grant can be accounted for?**

   A   Presented as a credit in the statement of profit or loss

   B   Presented as a credit in the statement of profit or loss, or deducted from the related expense

   C   Deducted from the related expense in the statement of profit or loss

   D   Deducted against the cost of the non-current asset

   E   Treat the grant as a deferred credit and transfer a portion to other income in the statement of profit or loss each year

3 **Intangible assets**

The following topics are covered in this chapter:
- Recognition and measurement
- Goodwill
- Research and development

3.1 RECOGNITION AND MEASUREMENT

LEARNING SUMMARY

After studying this section you should be able to:

- identify intangible assets
- understand how intangible assets can be recognised.

DEFINITION An **intangible asset** is 'an identifiable non-monetary asset without physical substance' (IAS 38, para 8).

Intangible assets can be purchased or internally generated, e.g. brand names.

KEY POINT As a general rule, purchased intangible assets are capitalised whereas internally generated intangible assets are not recognised in the financial statements.

- When the cost and expected useful life of an intangible asset can be reliably measured, they must be amortised to reflect the using up or wearing out of that asset.

- If the expected useful life cannot be reliably estimated, the intangible asset is subject to an annual impairment review, rather than an annual amortisation charge.

Amortisation is really the same as depreciation but a term used in relation to intangible assets.

Goodwill

Development costs

Trademarks

Examples of intangible assets

Brands

Licences

Copyrights

Recognition of intangible assets

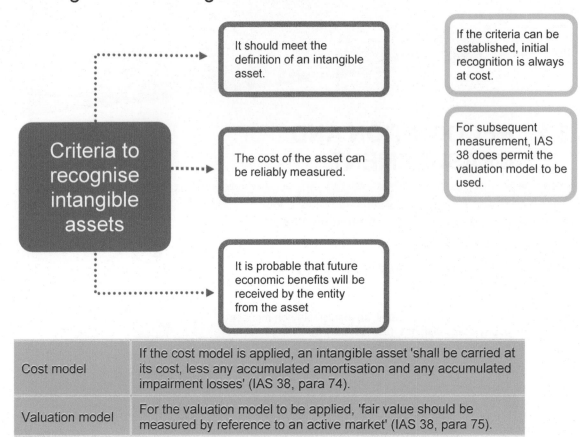

Cost model	If the cost model is applied, an intangible asset 'shall be carried at its cost, less any accumulated amortisation and any accumulated impairment losses' (IAS 38, para 74).
Valuation model	For the valuation model to be applied, 'fair value should be measured by reference to an active market' (IAS 38, para 75).

3.2 GOODWILL

LEARNING SUMMARY

After studying this section you should be able to:

- explain the accounting treatment of goodwill.

Calculation

Goodwill is the difference between the value of a business as a whole and the fair value of its identifiable net assets.

Purchased v non purchased

Purchased goodwill arises when an entity acquires a business (covered in Chapter 17).

KEY POINT Non-purchased, or inherent, goodwill is not recognised within the financial statements because it is not separable from the business.

Negative goodwill

Where an acquiring entity pays less for a business than the fair value of its separable net assets, the negative goodwill created is immediately recognised as income in the statement of profit or loss.

3.3 RESEARCH AND DEVELOPMENT

LEARNING SUMMARY

After studying this section you should be able to:

- differentiate between research and development expenditure
- outline the criteria that must be met to capitalise development expenditure.

Research

> **DEFINITION Research** is 'original and planned investigation undertaken with the prospect of gaining new scientific or technical knowledge and understanding' (IAS 38, para 8).

All research expenditure must be written off to the statement of profit or loss as it is incurred.

Development

> **DEFINITION Development** is 'the application of research findings or other knowledge to a plan or design for the production of new or substantially improved materials, devices, products, processes, systems or services before the start of commercial production or use' (IAS 38, para 8).

KEY POINT Development costs are a particular class of research expenditure that meets certain criteria and which therefore enables a separate accounting treatment to be applied to it.

Accounting treatment of development expenditure

Development costs must be capitalised as an intangible asset on the statement of financial position provided that all of the following criteria are met:

P	·······▶	Probable flow of economic benefit
I	·······▶	Intention to complete the project
R	·······▶	Reliable measurement of development cost
A	·······▶	Adequate resources available to complete the project
T	·······▶	Technically feasible
E	·······▶	Expected to be profitable

If the 'PIRATE' criteria are not met, development expenditure is treated as research activity.

KEY POINT Each project should be reviewed at the year-end to ensure that the 'PIRATE' criteria are still met. If they are no longer met, the previously capitalised expenditure must be written off to the statement of profit or loss immediately.

Do you understand?

1   Categorise the following non-current assets as tangible or intangible:

(i)   Land & buildings

(ii)   Motor vehicles

(iii)   Patents

(iv)   Licences.

2   Goodwill is most appropriately classified as a tangible non-current asset.

True or false?

3   TFZ Ltd has spent $100,000 investigating a chemical compound, known as NN4P and has found it is not harmful to mammals. Should this be classified as development costs?

4   Rihanna Ltd has incurred a further $250,000 using a specialised gel for creating prototypes of a new heat-resistant suit for stuntmen. Should this be classified as development costs?

1   (i) and (ii) are tangible non-current assets, (iii) and (iv) are intangible assets.

2   False. Goodwill is most appropriately classified as an intangible non-current asset.

3   No – this should not be classified as development as it has no form of commercial production in mind.

4   Yes – this should be classified as development as it has commercial production in mind.

20

1   Which of the following CANNOT be recognised as an intangible non-current asset in GHK's consolidated statement of financial position at 30 September 20X1?

A   GHK spent $132,000 developing a new type of product. In June 20X1 management worried that it would be too expensive to fund. The finances to complete the project came from a cash injection from a benefactor received in November 20X1.

B   GHK purchased a subsidiary during the year. During the fair value exercise, it was found that the subsidiary had a brand name with an estimated value of $50,000, but was not recognised by the subsidiary as it was internally generated.

C   GHK purchased a brand name from a competitor on 1 November 20X0, for $65,000.

D   GHK spent $21,000 during the year on the development of a new product, after management concluded it would be viable in November 20X0. The product is being launched on the market on 1 December 20X1 and is expected to be profitable.

2   Which of the following could be classified as development expenditure in M's statement of financial position as at 31 March 20Y0 according to IAS 38 Intangible Assets?

A $120,000 spent on developing a prototype and testing a new type of propulsion system. The project needs further work on it as the system is currently not viable.

B   A payment of $50,000 to a local university's engineering faculty to research new environmentally friendly building techniques.

C $35,000 developing an electric bicycle. This is near completion and the product will be launched soon. As this project is first of its kind it is expected to make a loss.

D $65,000 developing a special type of new packaging for a new energy efficient light bulb. The packaging is expected to reduce M's distribution costs by $35,000 a year.

3   Which TWO of the following factors is a reason why key staff cannot be capitalised as an intangible asset by an entity?

A   They do not provide expected future economic benefits

B   They cannot be controlled by an entity

C   Their value cannot be measured reliably

D   They are not separable from the business as a whole

4 Impairment of assets

The following topics are covered in this chapter:
- Impairment of individual assets
- Reversal of impairment
- Cash generating units

4.1 IMPAIRMENT OF INDIVIDUAL ASSETS

LEARNING SUMMARY

After studying this section you should be able to:

- define an impairment loss
- list the circumstances which may indicate impairment to assets
- understand the calculation used to determine whether an impairment exists
- explain the recognition and measurement of an impairment.

Calculation for impairment

KEY POINT An asset is impaired if its recoverable amount is below its carrying amount.

An asset's recoverable amount is the higher of its:

- fair value less costs to sell
- value in use: the present value of cash generated by the asset.

Indications of impairment

Internal	External
Evidence of obsolescence/damage	Decline in market value
Changes in asset use	Changes in environment: economic, market, technological or legal
Asset performance below expectations	Increased interest rates, reducing value in use

Recognition and measurement

KEY POINT If impaired, an asset should be written down to its recoverable amount and the impairment loss should be taken to the statement of profit or loss.

The only exception to this is where the asset has previously been revalued, in which case the impairment will first be taken to the revaluation surplus, via other comprehensive income. Any excess would then be taken to the statement of profit or loss.

4.2 REVERSAL OF IMPAIRMENT

LEARNING SUMMARY

After studying this section you should be able to:

- account for the reversal of an impairment loss on an individual asset.

Changes in recoverable amount

Sometimes the events anticipated to cause impairment of an asset turn out better than predicted. If this happens the recoverable amount is recalculated and the previous impairment reversed.

The reversal is recognised immediately in the statement of profit or loss. If the previous impairment was charged against the revaluation surplus, then the reversal is recognised as other comprehensive income and credited to the revaluation surplus.

The reversal must not increase the value of the asset above its depreciated original cost i.e. the value that it would have had if no impairment had been recorded.

4.3   CASH GENERATING UNITS

LEARNING SUMMARY

After studying this section you should be able to:

- describe a cash generating unit (CGU)

- allocate an impairment loss to the assets of a CGU.

DEFINITION A **cash generating unit** is the smallest identifiable group of assets for which independent cash flows are identifiable.

For example, within a college, independent cashflows are not identifiable for each piece of furniture, or maybe even all the furniture within each classroom, and it is necessary to combine all the assets at a particular location to identify the independent cashflows.

Impairment calculation

KEY POINT The assets in the CGU are grouped together and their combined value is compared to the total recoverable amount.

Impairment exists where the total carrying amount is greater than the total recoverable amount.

The calculated total impairment needs to be allocated against specific assets.

Having impaired any specifically impaired items, assets should be impaired in the following order:

1   Purchased goodwill

2   Remaining assets pro-rata based on their carrying amount.

> Remember that no asset can be written down below its recoverable amount.

Do you understand?

1   How is recoverable amount calculated?

2   How is an impairment calculated?

1   Recoverable amount is calculated by taking the higher of fair value less costs to sell and value in use.
2   An impairment is calculated by comparing carrying value to the recoverable amount. An impairment exists where carrying value is greater than the recoverable amount.

OT Case – practice

Desert owns and operates an item of plant that cost $640,000 and had accumulated depreciation of $400,000 at 1 October 20X4. It is being depreciated at 12.5% per annum on cost. On 1 April 20X5 the plant was damaged when a factory vehicle collided into it.

Based on the damage, the estimated value of the plant in use is $150,000. The plant has a current disposal value of $20,000, but Desert has been offered a trade-in value of $180,000 if it upgrades, which Desert is unlikely to do.

Desert also sold bottled water, and the assets in the water division are:

	$000
Brand (Quencher – see below)	7,000
Land containing spa	12,000
Purifying and bottling plant	8,000

During the year, the water became contaminated and Desert' reputation was affected. It is estimated that the division is worth $15 million in total.

Due to the reputational damage, the Quencher brand is now deemed to be worthless.

1   **Which of the following statements regarding impairment is correct?**

   A   The recoverable amount is the lower of the fair value less costs to sell and the value in use

   B   An asset is impaired if the carrying amount is higher than the recoverable amount

   C   The value in use represents the price in an arms-length transaction

   D   Impairment losses should always be taken to the statement of profit or loss

2   **What is the carrying amount of Desert's plant immediately before the impairment?**

   A $200,000

   B $150,000

   C $180,000

   D $240,000

3   **What is the recoverable amount of Desert's plant at the date of the impairment?**

   A $200,000

   B $150,000

   C $180,000

   D $20,000

4 **What is the value of the bottling plant following the impairment review?**

    A $8,000,000

    B $6,000,000

    C $5,500,000

    D $5,000,000

5 **Identify which of the assets below require an annual impairment review.**

    (i)   Intangible assets with an indefinite life

    (ii)   Land with an indefinite life

    A   (i) only

    B   (ii) only

    C   Both (i) and (ii)

    D   Neither of the assets

Non-current assets held for sale and discontinued operations

The following topics are covered in this chapter:
- Assets held for sale
- Discontinued operations

5.1 ASSETS HELD FOR SALE

LEARNING SUMMARY

After studying this section you should be able to:

- account for non-current assets held for sale.

DEFINITION An **asset held for sale** is one where the carrying amount of the asset will be recovered primarily from a sales transaction rather than continuing use (IFRS 5).

Recognition and measurement

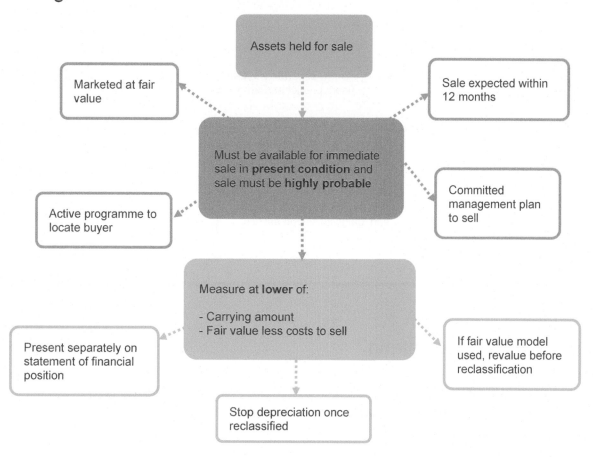

5.2 DISCONTINUED OPERATIONS

After studying this section you should be able to:

* account for discontinued operations.

Accounting treatment

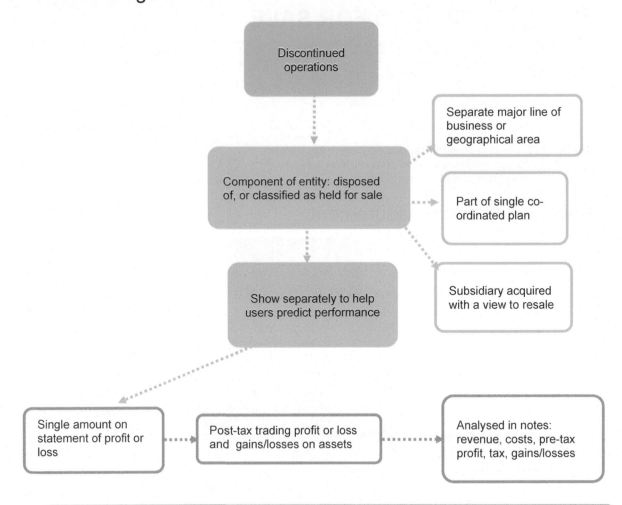

Do you understand?

1   How are assets held for sale presented in the financial statements?

2   An asset held for sale will be depreciated until it is sold.
     True or false?

3   How are discontinued operations presented in the financial statements?

Pro-forma statement of profit or loss

	$
Revenue	X
Cost of sales	(X)
Gross profit	X
Distribution costs	(X)
Administrative expenses	(X)
Profit from operations	X
Investment income	X
Finance costs	(X)
Profit before tax	X
Tax expense	(X)
Profit for the period from continuing operations	X
Discontinued operations:	
Profit for the period from discontinued operations	X
Total profit for the period	X

1   AB has an asset that was classed as held for sale at 31 March 20X2. The asset had a carrying amount of $900 and a fair value of $800. The cost of disposal was estimated to be $50.

According to IFRS 5 *Non-current Assets Held for Sale and Discontinued Operations*, which value should be used for the asset as at 31 March 20X2?

A $750

B $800

C $850

D $900

2   **According to IFRS 5 *Non-current Assets Held for Sale and Discontinued Operations* which of the following relate to the criteria for an asset held for sale?**

(i)   Available for immediate sale in its present condition

(ii)   Sale is highly probable

(iii)   The sale is expected to be completed within the next month

(iv)   A reasonable price has been set

A   All of the above

B   (i), (ii) and (iii)

C   (i), (ii) and (iv)

D   (ii), (iii) and (iv)

3   **According to IFRS 5 *Non-current Assets Held for Sale and Discontinued Operations* which of the following amounts in respect of a discontinued operation must be shown on the face of the statement of profit or loss?**

	Shown on the face of the statement of profit or loss	Not shown
Revenue		
Gross profit		
Profit after tax		

4   Total Co has the following two lines of business that have been disposed of in the year:

Sector X operated in Country A. Total Co has no other operations in Country A, and Country A made up 0.5% of the total revenue of Total Co.

Sector Y operated in the same country as the Total Co head office. It produced a different item from the other parts of total Co, and this item contributed 10% of the total revenue of Total Co.

Which of these sectors, if any, should be disclosed as a discontinued operation in the current year?

	Discontinued operation Yes/No
Sector X	
Sector Y	

6.1 REGULATORY FRAMEWORK

LEARNING SUMMARY

After studying this section you should be able to:

- outline the standard setting process

- explain why a regulatory framework is required

- distinguish between a principles-based and a rules-based framework.

International Financial Reporting Standards Foundation (the Foundation) Responsible for governance of the IFRS Standard setting process	**International Financial Reporting Standards Board (the Board)** Responsible for setting IFRS Standards
IFRS® Interpretations Committee (IFRIC®) Issues guidance where divergent interpretations have arisen	**IFRS Advisory Council** Forum for experts to offer advice to the Board

Why a framework is needed

To ensure the achievement of relevant and reliable financial reporting in order to meet the needs of users.

Full regulation of financial statement preparation cannot be achieved by accounting standards alone. Additional control is required in the form of legal and market regulations.

Principles-based vs rules-based accounting

Principles-based accounting	Rules-based accounting
Follows a conceptual framework, such as the Board's Framework.	Accounting standards are a set of rules to be followed.
Accounting standards are created based on the conceptual framework.	Often described as a 'cookbook' approach.

Standard setting process

> The Board identifies a subject requiring a new standard

> The Board establishes an Advisory Committee to recommend appropriate treatment

> An Exposure Draft is issued for public comment

> Having considered comments received, the Board publishes the standard.

National standard setters

Committed to a framework of standards based on IFRS Standards.

Trend towards harmonisation means national standards are unlikely to be produced that conflict with IFRS Standards.

6.2   CONCEPTUAL FRAMEWORK

LEARNING SUMMARY

After studying this section you should be able to:

- define fundamental and enhancing qualitative characteristics

- define and explain recognition in financial statements, applying the recognition criteria to assets, liabilities, income and expenses.

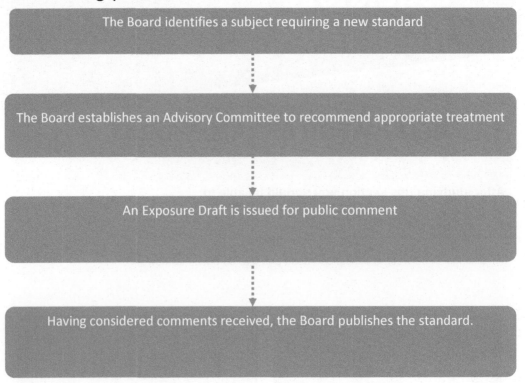

Qualitative characteristics

Fundamental → Relevance / Faithful representation

Enhancing → Comparability / Verifiability / Timeliness / Understandability

Fundamental qualitative characteristics	
Relevance	It influences the economic decisions of users by helping them evaluate past, present or future events or confirming or correcting their past evaluations.
Faithful representation	Transactions and other events must be accounted for and presented in accordance with their substance and economic reality and not merely their legal form.
Enhancing qualitative characteristics	
Comparability	Users must be able to compare financial statements over a period of time to identify trends and to compare financial statements of different entities to be able to assess their relative financial position and performance.
Verifiability	Can be direct or indirect. Direct verification means verifying through direct observation. Indirect verification means checking the inputs to a model, formula or other technique and recalculating the outputs using the same methodology.
Timeliness	Information made available to decision makers in time to be capable of influencing their decisions .
Understandability	Readily understandable by users, although relevant information should never be excluded due to being considered too difficult for some users.

Elements of the financial statements

KEY POINT The financial statements must summarise five key elements in order to reflect the financial position and performance.

Statement of profit or loss	Statement of financial position
Income	Assets
Expense	Liability
	Equity

It is important to know which elements appear in each of the financial statements.

DEFINITION An **asset** is 'a resource owned or controlled by an entity as a result of past events and from which future economic benefits are expected to flow to the entity' (Framework, Glossary)

DEFINITION A **liability** is 'a present obligation arising from past events, the settlement of which is expected to result in an outflow from the entity of resources embodying economic benefits' (Framework, Glossary)

These definitions could be tested as part of an objective test question.

DEFINITION **Capital/equity** is a special kind of liability due to the owner(s) and is 'the residual interest in the assets of the entity after deducting all its liabilities' (Framework, para 4.4)

Recognition

In order to be recognised, an item that meets the definition of an element must also meet the following criteria:

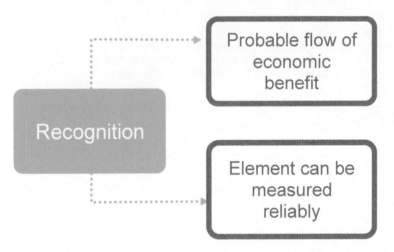

Recognition → Probable flow of economic benefit

Recognition → Element can be measured reliably

Do you understand?

1   The International Financial Reporting Standards Foundation is responsible for setting the IFRS Standards.

     True or false?

2   Accounting standards are a set of rules to be followed.

     True or false?

3   Faithful representation means that the commercial effect of a transaction must always be shown in the financial statements even if this differs from legal form.

     True or false?

1   False. The International Financial Reporting Standards Board is responsible for setting IFRS Standards.
2   True.
3   True. Faithful representation includes the concept that transactions should reflect their economic substance, rather than the legal form of the transaction.

Exam style questions

1   Which one of the following statements best defines a liability?

   A   A liability is an obligation arising from a past transaction or event.

   B   A liability is a legally binding amount owed to a third party.

   C   A liability is an obligation arising from a past transaction or event which is expected to be settled by an outflow of economic benefits.

   D   A liability is anything which results in an outflow of economic benefits from an entity.

2   Which one of the following statements best defines an asset?

   A   An asset is a resource owned by the entity with a financial value.

   B   An asset is a resource controlled by an entity from which future economic benefits are expected to be generated.

   C   An asset is a resource controlled by an entity as a result of past events.

   D   An asset is a resource controlled by an entity as a result of past events from which future economic benefits are expected to be generated.

3   Which of the following items is not an enhancing qualitative characteristic of useful financial information as stated in the IASB Framework?

   A   Comparability

   B   Timeliness

   C   Faithful representation

   D   Understandability

4   Which two of the following items are enhancing qualitative characteristics as stated in the IASB Framework?

   A   Relevance

   B   Comparability

   C   Faithful representation

   D   Verifiability

7.1 MEASUREMENT

LEARNING SUMMARY

After studying this section you should be able to:

- explain the use of historical cost, current cost, realisable value and present value

- discuss the advantages and disadvantages of historical cost accounting.

The IASB® Conceptual Framework (the Framework) lists the following measurement bases:

Historical cost	**Current cost**
Items are recorded at the amount of consideration given at the time of acquisition	Items are carried at the value to be paid to acquire the equivalent item currently

Realisable value	**Present value**
Items are carried at the amount that could be obtained from an orderly disposal	Items are carried at the discounted present value of future cash flows relating to the item

Advantages of financial statements produced using historical cost

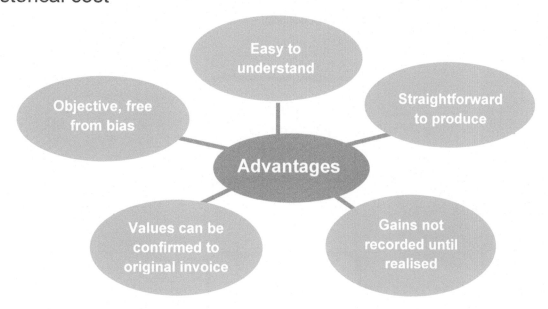

Disadvantages of financial statements produced using historical cost

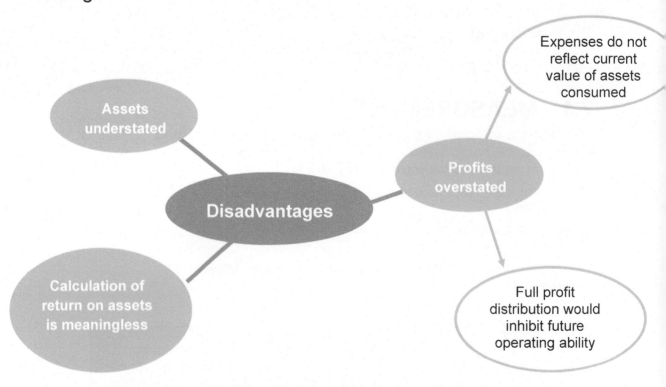

7.2 CAPITAL MAINTENANCE

LEARNING SUMMARY

After studying this section you should be able to:

- describe the concept of financial and physical capital maintenance and how this affects the determination of profits.

Alternative to historical cost accounting

There are two main forms of current value accounting which seek to tackle the disadvantages of historical cost accounting.

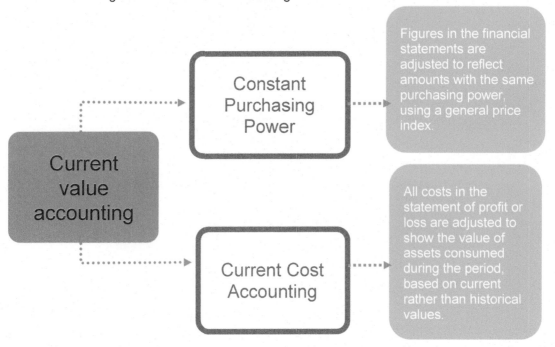

Capital

An entity can adopt financial or physical concepts for capital.

Financial

- Capital is viewed as amounts invested (in either historical cost or purchasing power terms).
- Financial capital maintenance seeks to preserve the value of shareholders' funds, either in monetary terms (historical cost) or real terms (constant purchasing power).

Physical

- Capital is viewed as the productive capacity of an entity.
- Physical capital maintenance seeks to preserve sufficient shareholders' funds to allow the business to continue to operate at current levels of activity, achieved by some form of CCA, adjusting for specific price changes.

Do you understand?

1 Current cost is where items are carried at the amount that could be obtained from an orderly disposal.

True or false?

2 One of the advantages of historical cost accounting is that profits are overstated.

True or false?

3 Under which concept is capital viewed as amounts invested?

Financial concept or physical concept?

1 False. Realisable value is where items are carried at the amount that could be obtained from an orderly disposal.

2 False. This is one of the disadvantages.

3 Capital is viewed as amounts invested under the physical concept.

1   **Which of the following is not a measurement base referred to in the IASB's Conceptual Framework?**

A   Current cost

B   Residual value

C   Historical cost

D   Present value

2   **Which of the following concepts measures profits in terms of an increase in the productive capacity of an entity?**

Which one of the following statements best defines a liability?

A   Physical capital maintenance

B   Historical cost accounting

C   Financial capital maintenance

D   Going concern concept

3   **Which one of the following statements is true about historical cost accounts in times of rising prices?**

A   Profits will be overstated and assets will be understated

B   Asset values will be overstated

C   Unrecognised gains will be recorded incorrectly

D   Depreciation will be overstated

8 Other standards

The following topics are covered in this chapter:

- IAS 8 *Accounting policies, changes in accounting estimates and errors*
- IFRS 13 *Fair value measurement*
- IAS 2 *Inventories*
- IAS 41 *Agriculture*

8.1 IAS 8 *ACCOUNTING POLICIES, CHANGES IN ACCOUNTING ESTIMATES AND ERRORS*

LEARNING SUMMARY

After studying this section you should be able to:

- account for changes in accounting estimates, changes in accounting policy and correction of prior period errors.

DEFINITION **Accounting policies** are the specific principles, bases, conventions, rules and practices applied by an entity in preparing and presenting financial statements (IAS 8, para 5).

Selection of accounting policies

IAS 8 requires an entity to select and apply appropriate accounting policies to ensure that the information in financial statements

- is relevant to the decision-making needs of users, and
- faithfully represents the entity's performance and position.

Changes in accounting policy

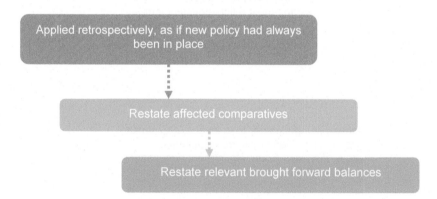

Applied retrospectively, as if new policy had always been in place

Restate affected comparatives

Restate relevant brought forward balances

Changes in accounting estimate

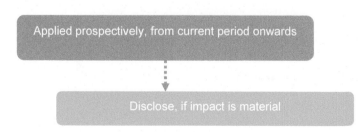

Applied prospectively, from current period onwards

Disclose, if impact is material

An example of a change in accounting estimate would be a change in the estimated useful life of a non-current asset.

Errors

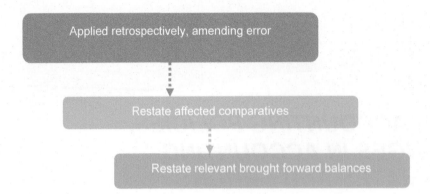

Applied retrospectively, amending error

Restate affected comparatives

Restate relevant brought forward balances

8.2 IFRS 13 *FAIR VALUE MEASUREMENT*

LEARNING SUMMARY

After studying this section you should be able to:

- explain and compute amounts using fair value.

DEFINITION Fair value is the price that would be received to sell an asset or paid to transfer a liability in an orderly transaction between market participants (IFRS 13, para 9).

Hierarchy of inputs

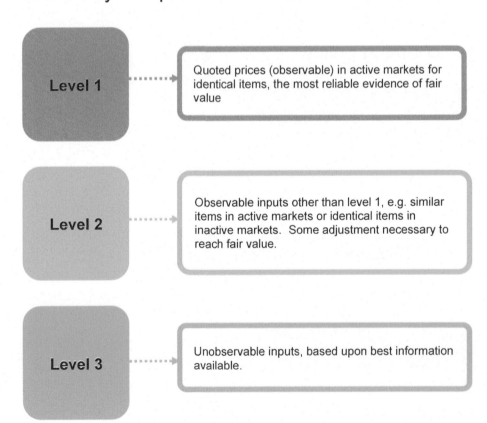

Level 1   Quoted prices (observable) in active markets for identical items, the most reliable evidence of fair value

Level 2   Observable inputs other than level 1, e.g. similar items in active markets or identical items in inactive markets. Some adjustment necessary to reach fair value.

Level 3   Unobservable inputs, based upon best information available.

You need to learn the hierarchy of inputs.

8.3 IAS 2 *INVENTORIES*

Valuation

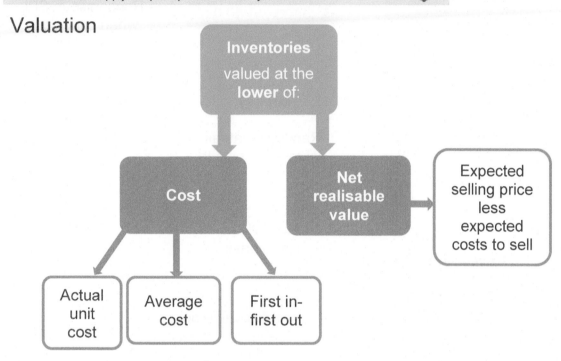

8.4 IAS 41 *AGRICULTURE*

Recognition and measurement

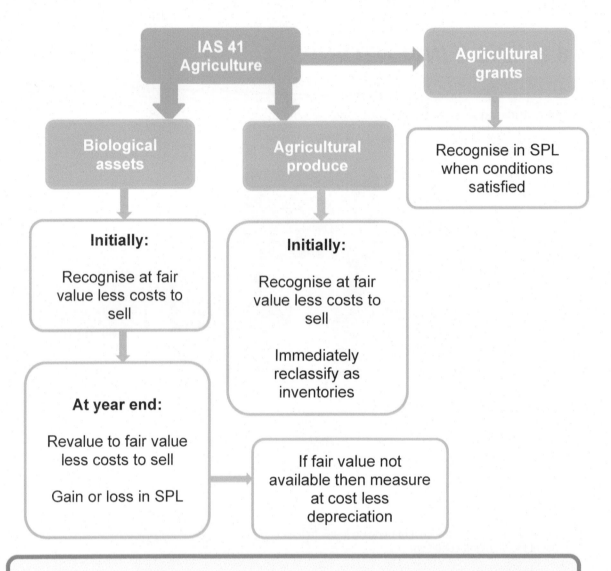

IAS 41 Agriculture

→ Agricultural grants

Biological assets

Agricultural produce

Recognise in SPL when conditions satisfied

Biological assets

Initially:

Recognise at fair value less costs to sell

At year end:

Revalue to fair value less costs to sell

Gain or loss in SPL

Agricultural produce

Initially:

Recognise at fair value less costs to sell

Immediately reclassify as inventories

If fair value not available then measure at cost less depreciation

Do you understand?

1   In accordance with IAS 8 Accounting Policies, Changes in Accounting Estimates and Errors how is a change in accounting estimate accounted for?

2   Level 1 inputs comprise quoted prices in active markets for identical assets and liabilities at the reporting date.

     True or false?

3   State the accounting treatment for agricultural grants.

1   By changing the current year figures but not the previous years' figures.
2   True.
3   Agricultural grants should be recognised in the Statement of Profit or Loss.

1   Which of the following is a change of accounting policy under
    IAS 8 *Accounting Policies, Changes in Accounting Estimates
    and Errors*?

	Change in accounting policy	Change in accounting estimate
Classifying commission earned as revenue in the statement of profit or loss, having previously classified it as other operating income		
Revising the remaining useful life of a depreciable asset		

2   Nina has only two items of inventory on hand at its reporting date.

    Item 1 – Materials costing $24,000 bought for processing and
    assembly for a customer under a 'one off' order which is expected to
    produce a high profit margin. Since buying this material, the cost price
    has fallen to $20,000.

    Item 2 – A machine constructed for another customer for a contracted
    price of $36,000. This has recently been completed at a cost of
    $33,600. It has now been discovered that, in order to meet certain
    health and safety regulations, modifications at an extra cost of $8,400
    will be required. The customer has agreed to meet half the extra cost.

    **What should be the total value of these two items of inventory in
    the statement of financial position?**

    $_____

3   Magna owned cattle recorded in the financial statements at $10,500
    on 1 January. At 31 December, the cattle has a fair value of $13,000.
    If Magna sold the cattle, commission of 2% would be payable.

    **What is the correct accounting treatment for the cattle at
    31 December according to IAS 41 *Agriculture*?**

    A   Hold at cost of $10,500

    B   Revalue to $13,000, taking gain of $2,500 to the statement of
        profit or loss

    C   Revalue to $13,000, taking gain of $2,500 to the revaluation
        surplus

    D   Revalue to $12,740, taking gain of $2,240 to the statement of
        profit or loss

9 Leases

The following topics are covered in this chapter:

- Definitions
- Lessee accounting
- Sale and leaseback

9.1 DEFINITIONS

LEARNING SUMMARY

After studying this section you should be able to:

- state the definitions of relevant terms.

> IFRS 16 is a new standard and therefore highly examinable.

DEFINITION A **lease** is a contract that conveys the right to use an underlying asset for a period of time in exchange for consideration (IFRS16, Appendix A).

DEFINITION The **lessor** is the entity that provides the right to use an underlying asset in exchange for consideration (IFRS 16, Appendix A).

DEFINITION The **lessee** is the entity that obtains the right to use an underlying asset in exchange for consideration (IFRS 16, Appendix A).

DEFINITION A **right-of-use** asset represents a lessee's right to use an underlying asset for the lease term (IFRS 16, Appendix A).

9.2 LESSEE ACCOUNTING

LEARNING SUMMARY

After studying this section you should be able to:

- account for right-of-use assets and lease liabilities in the records of the lessee.

Measurement

```
          ┌──────────────────┐
          │  At inception    │
          │    of lease      │
          │   recognise      │
          └──────────────────┘
           ↙              ↘
┌──────────────────┐  ┌──────────────────┐
│  Lease liability │  │  Right-of-use    │
│                  │  │     asset        │
└──────────────────┘  └──────────────────┘
```

Lease liability

Recognise at present value of payments not yet made:

- Fixed payments

- Amounts expected to be paid under residual value guarantees

- Options to purchase that are reasonably certain to be exercised

- Termination penalties if lease term reflects expectation that they will be incurred

Right-of-use asset

Recognise at cost, which equals:

- Initial value of lease liability

- Payments made at or before commencement

- Initial direct costs

- Estimated costs of asset removal or dismantling as per lease conditions

To calculate the lease liability and right-of-use asset entities must establish the length of the lease term. The lease term comprises

- Non-cancellable periods

- Periods covered by an option to extend the lease if reasonably certain to be exercised

- Periods covered by an option to terminate the lease if reasonably certain not to be exercised.

Subsequent measurement: liability

The liability is increased by the interest charge, which is also recorded in the statement of profit or loss:	
Dr	Finance costs
Cr	Lease liability
Cash payments reduce the lease liability:	
Dr	Lease liability
Cr	Cash

Subsequent measurement: right-of-use asset

Unless another model is chosen, the cost model is used. The asset will be measured at cost less accumulated depreciation and impairment losses.

The asset is depreciated:

- if ownership transfers to the lessee at the end of the lease, over the remaining useful economic life of the asset

- if ownership does not transfer to the lessee at the end of the lease, over the shorter of the lease term and the useful economic life of the asset.

Short-life and low value assets

If the lease is short-term (less than 12 months at the inception date) or of a low value then a simplified treatment is allowed.

In these cases, the lessee can choose to recognise the lease payments in profit or loss on a straight line basis. No lease liability or right-of-use asset would therefore be recognised.

9.3   SALE AND LEASEBACK

LEARNING SUMMARY

After studying this section you should be able to:

- account for sale and leaseback arrangements.

Is the transfer a 'sale'?

If an entity (the seller-lessee) transfers an asset to another entity (the buyer-lessor) and then leases it back, the seller-lessee must assess whether the transfer should be accounted for as a sale.

Entities must apply IFRS 15 Revenue from Contracts with Customers (see Chapter 12) to decide whether a performance obligation has been satisfied.

Accounting treatment

Transfer is not a sale	Transfer is a sale
Continue to recognise asset. Recognise a financial liability equal to proceeds received.	Derecognise the asset. Recognise a right-of-use asset as the proportion of the previous carrying amount that relates to the rights retained. Recognise a lease liability. A profit or loss on disposal will arise.

Do you understand?

1   A lease liability should be recognised at the expected costs to be paid in the future.

    True or false?

2   When establishing a lease term, the period covered by an option to extend the lease if reasonably certain not to be exercised should be included.

    True or false?

3   What is the double entry for recording the interest charge?

1   False. A lease liability should be recognised at the present value of payments not yet made.
2   False. It will be included where the periods covered by an option to extend the lease if it is reasonably certain to be exercised.
3   The double entry is Dr Finance costs Cr Lease liability.

NOTE: Due to the nature of objective case questions, the following questions may also test areas of the syllabus included in other chapters.

Section B type question - practice

On 1 October 20X6 Fino entered into an agreement to lease twenty telephones for its team of sales staff. The telephones are to be leased for a period of 24 months at a cost of $240 per telephone per annum, payable annually in advance. The present value of the lease payments at 1 October 20X6 is $9,164.

On 1 April 20X7, Fino entered into an agreement to lease an item of plant from the manufacturer. The lease required four annual payments in advance of $100,000 each commencing on 1 April 20X7. The plant would have a useful life of four years and would be scrapped at the end of this period. The present value of the total lease payments is $350,000.

Fino has a cost of capital of 10%.

1   **Which of the following applies the principle of faithful representation to the above lease agreement?**

    A   Recording an annual rent expense in Fino's statement of profit or loss

    B   Expensing any interest on a straight-line basis over 4 years

    C   Recording an asset in Fino's statement of financial position to reflect control

    D   Record the $100,000 paid as a prepayment to be released over 4 years

2   **How much would be charged to Fino's statement of profit or loss for the year ended 30 September 20X7 in respect of the telephones?**

    A $4,800

    B $4,582

    C $4,364

    D $5,498

3   **What would be the carrying amount of the leased plant as at 30 September 20X7?**

    $_____

4   **What interest would be charged to Fino's statement of profit or loss for the year ended 30 September 20X7 in respect of the plant lease?**

    A $12,500

    B $25,000

    C $17,500

    D $35,000

5   Applying the principles of IFRS 16 Leases to capitalise the plant
        and recognise the lease liability would have what impact upon
        the following ratios?

	Increase	Decrease
Return on Capital Employed		
Gearing		
Interest cover		

10 Financial assets and financial liabilities

The following topics are covered in this chapter:

- Financial instruments
- Financial liabilities
- Compound instruments
- Financial assets
- Derecognition
- Factoring

10.1 FINANCIAL INSTRUMENTS

LEARNING SUMMARY

After studying this section you should be able to:

- define financial instruments in terms of financial assets and financial liabilities.

DEFINITION A **financial instrument** is a contract that gives rise to a financial asset of one entity and a financial liability or equity instrument of another entity (IAS 32, para 11).

DEFINITION A **financial asset** is:

- Cash
- An equity instrument of another entity
- A contractual right to receive cash or another financial asset
- A contractual right to exchange financial assets or liabilities on favourable terms.

  (IAS 32, para 11)

> Learn these definitions as they could be tested as an objective test question.

DEFINITION A **financial liability** is:

- A contractual obligation to deliver cash or another financial asset
- A contractual obligation to exchange financial assets or liabilities on unfavourable terms.

  (IAS 32, para 11)

Debt or equity?

KEY POINT When issuing finance, an entity must classify it as a financial liability or as equity according to its substance.

The decision as to whether a financial instrument is a financial liability or equity has a big impact on the financial statements.

KEY POINT The treatment of interest and dividends relating to a financial instrument must also follow the treatment of the instrument itself.

10.2 FINANCIAL LIABILITIES

Categories

Financial liabilities

Amortised cost

Used for most financial liabilities

Fair value through profit or loss

Used for liabilities held for trading or derivatives

Amortised cost

The accounting treatment of financial liabilities measured at amortised cost is as follows:

They are initially recognised at fair value (normally the proceeds received) less any transaction costs (such as legal or broker fees).

They are subsequently measured at amortised cost:

- interest is charged to profit or loss using the effective rate and is added on to the carrying amount of the liability

- any cash payments during the year are deducted from the carrying amount of the liability.

The effective rate of interest spreads all of the costs of the liability (such as transaction fees, issue discounts, annual interest payments and redemption premiums) to profit or loss over the term of the instrument.

The following table is useful for working out the carrying amount of a liability that is measured at amortised cost:

Reporting period	Opening amount	Interest[2]	Cash[3]	Closing amount
Year ended 31 December 20X1	X[1]	X	(X)	X

[1] In the first year of the liability, the initial value will be its fair value less transaction costs.

[2] Interest is charged using the effective rate of interest.

[3] Cash interest payments are normally based on the nominal (par) value of the liability and the coupon rate of interest.

> Check the question for dates as you may not need to prepare the table for the full length of the contract.

10.3 COMPOUND INSTRUMENTS

Substance over form

KEY POINT A compound instrument is one that has characteristics of both a financial liability and equity.

A common example is the issue of a bond or loan that allows the holders the choice of redemption in the form of cash or a fixed number of equity shares.

IAS 32 specifies that compound instruments must be split into:

- a liability component (the obligation to repay cash)

- an equity component (the obligation to issue a fixed number of shares).

Split accounting

The split of the liability component and the equity component at the issue date is calculated as follows:

- the liability component is the present value of the cash repayments, discounted using the market rate for non-convertible bonds

- the equity component is the difference between the cash received and the liability component at the issue date.

KEY POINT After initial recognition, the liability will be measured at amortised cost. The equity component is not remeasured and remains unchanged.

10.4 FINANCIAL ASSETS

Classification and measurement: investments in shares

```
┌─────────────────────┐
│   Investments in    │
│  shares (equity)    │
└─────────────────────┘
```

```
┌──────────────────────┐      ┌──────────────────────┐
│     Fair Value       │      │     Fair Value       │
│     through          │      │   through Other      │
│   Statement of       │      │   Comprehensive      │
│  Profit and Loss     │      │      Income          │
│                      │      │                      │
│   Default position   │      │    If not held for   │
│                      │      │  short-term trading  │
│                      │      │   and an irrevocable │
│                      │      │   designation is     │
│                      │      │       made.          │
└──────────────────────┘      └──────────────────────┘
```

```
┌──────────────────────┐      ┌──────────────────────┐
│ Initial recognition: │      │ Initial recognition: │
│ Fair value (costs    │      │ Fair value plus costs│
│ written off to       │      │                      │
│ Statement of Profit  │      │ Subsequent treatment:│
│ or Loss)             │      │ Revalue each         │
│                      │      │ reporting date with  │
│ Subsequent treatment:│      │ gain or loss in      │
│ Revalue each         │      │ Other Comprehensive  │
│ reporting date with  │      │ Income               │
│ gain or loss in      │      │                      │
│ Statement of Profit  │      │                      │
│ or Loss              │      │                      │
└──────────────────────┘      └──────────────────────┘
```

Classification: investments in debt

IFRS 9 specifies three ways of classifying debt investments:

- Amortised cost
- Fair value through other comprehensive income
- Fair value through profit or loss.

A financial asset is measured at amortised cost if:

- the objective of the business model within which the asset is held is to hold the asset to maturity to collect the contractual cash flows
- the contractual terms of the asset give rise to cash flows that are solely repayments of principal and interest of the principal amount outstanding. Interest payments should offer adequate compensation for risk and the time value of money.

A financial asset is measured at fair value through other comprehensive income if:

- the objective of the business model within which the asset is held is to both collect contractual cash flows but also to increase returns when possible by selling the asset

- the contractual terms of the asset give rise to cash flows that are solely repayments of principal and interest of the principal amount outstanding.

If not classified as one of the above two categories, the financial asset is measured at fair value through profit or loss.

Measurement: investments in debt

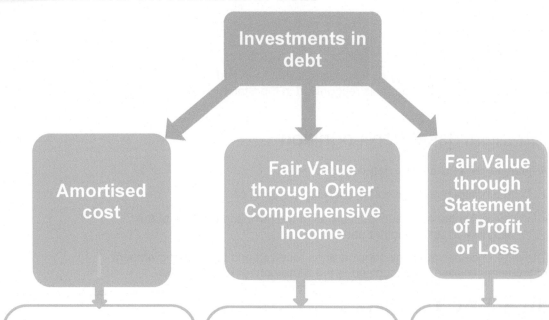

10.5 DERECOGNITION

Financial liability derecognition

A financial liability should be derecognised when the obligation is extinguished. This may happen when the contract:

* is discharged, or

* is cancelled, or

* expires.

The difference between any consideration transferred and the carrying amount of the financial liability is recognised in the Statement of Profit or Loss.

Financial asset derecognition

A financial asset should be derecognised when:

* the contractual rights to the cash flows expire, or

* the entity transfers substantially all of the risks and rewards of the financial asset to another party.

The difference between any consideration received and the carrying amount of the financial asset is recognised in the Statement of Profit or Loss.

10.6 FACTORING

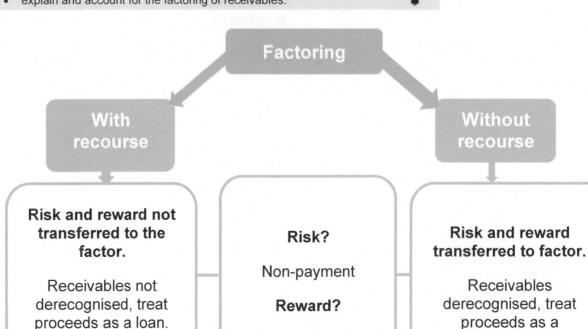

Do you understand?

1   In respect of shares classified as a liability, how are dividends paid reflected in the financial statements?

2   When financial liabilities are issued, the legal or broker fees are charged as a cost through the Statement of Profit or Loss.

   True or false?

3   Under split accounting, explain how the liability component is calculated for a compound instrument.

1   Viking issues $100,000 5% loan notes on 1 January 20X4, incurring issue costs of $3,000. These loan notes are redeemable at a premium, meaning that the effective rate of interest is 8% per annum.

What is the finance cost to be shown in the statement of profit or loss for the year ended 31 December 20X5?

A $8,240

B $7,981

C $7,760

D $8,000

2   **What is the default classification for an equity investment?**

A   Fair value through profit or loss

B   Fair value through other comprehensive income

C   Amortised cost

D   Net proceeds

3   **For which category of financial instruments are transaction costs excluded from the initial value, and instead expensed to profit or loss?**

A   Financial liabilities at amortised cost

B   Financial assets at fair value through profit or loss

C   Financial assets at fair value through other comprehensive income

D   Financial assets at amortised cost

11.1 CURRENCY

LEARNING SUMMARY

After studying this section you should be able to:

- define presentation and functional currencies.

DEFINITION **Functional currency** is 'the currency of the primary economic environment in which an entity operates' (IAS 21, para 8).

DEFINITION **Presentation currency** is 'the currency in which the financial statements are presented' (IAS 21, para 8).

Factors influencing functional currency:

- the currency that influences sales prices
- the currency that influences labour, material and other costs.

11.2 TRANSLATING TRANSACTIONS

LEARNING SUMMARY

After studying this section you should be able to:

- record transactions in a foreign currency.

Initial transactions and settlements

KEY POINT Overseas transactions must be translated into the entity's functional currency before they are recorded.

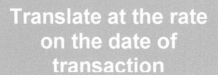

Initial transaction

⬇

Translate at the rate on the date of transaction

The foreign exchange gain or loss will be recorded in the statement of profit or loss.

KEY POINT If exchange rates have moved between the initial transaction and the settlement date then a foreign exchange gain or loss will arise

Unsettled balances at the reporting date

Monetary items include receivables, payables and loans.

Reporting date

Monetary items
Retranslate using the
closing rate of
exchange.
Exchange gains or
losses to the SPL.

**Non-monetary
items**
Do not re-translate.
If held at fair value then
the fair value should be
translated using the rate
on the revaluation date.

Do you understand?

1   Swati has a year end of 31 December and uses the dollar ($) as its functional currency.

On 1 December 20X8 Swati purchased goods on credit from an overseas supplier, whose functional currency is the Dinar (D). The goods were priced at D60,000 and the supplier allowed Swati 60 days' credit.

Rates of exchange were as follows:

1   December 20X8 $1 = D1.50

31 December 20X8 $1 = D1.80

Record the journals for this transaction for the year ended 31 December 20X8.

---

1.   1 December 20X8 Purchase
Value of goods = D60,000 @ 1.50 = $40,000

	$	$
Dr Purchases	40,000	
Cr Payables		40,000

31 December 20X8 retranslate payables (monetary item) at closing rate.
D60,000 @ 1.80 = $33,333. Exchange difference of $6,667 reduces payables balance and is credited to statement of profit or loss.

	$	$
Dr Payables	6,667	
Cr SPL: Exchange gain		6,667

---

1 IAS 21 *The Effects of Changes in Foreign Exchange Rates* defines the term 'functional currency'.

   Which one of the following is the correct definition of 'functional currency'?

   A   The currency in which the financial statements are presented

   B   The currency of the country where the reporting entity is located

   C   The currency that mainly influences sales prices and operating costs

   D   The currency of the primary economic environment in which an entity operates

2 Moonlight is a public limited company with a reporting date of 31 December 20X1 and a functional currency of dollars ($).On 30 June 20X1, it purchased land from overseas at a cost of 30 million dinars. The land is an item of property, plant and equipment and is measured using the cost model.

   Exchange rates are as follows:

	Dinars: $1
30/6/20X1	3
31/12/20X1	2
Average rate for year-ended 31/12/20X1	2.5

   The fair value of the land at 31 December 20X1 was 32 million dinars.

   What is the carrying amount of the land as at 31 December 20X1?

   A $10 million

   B $15 million

   C $12 million

   D $16 million

The following topics are covered in this chapter:
- Revenue recognition
- Statement of financial position

12.1 REVENUE RECOGNITION

LEARNING SUMMARY

After studying this section you should be able to:

- explain and apply the five step model that relates to revenue earned from a contract with a customer

- explain and apply the revenue recognition criteria where performance obligations are satisfied over time or at a point in time

- describe acceptable methods for measuring progress towards performance obligation satisfaction.

DEFINITION **Revenue** is 'income arising in the course of an entity's ordinary activities' (IFRS 15, Appendix A).

IFRS 15 *Revenue from Contracts with Customers* specifies a five-step approach to recognition of revenue:

Step 1
Identify the Contract with the customer

Step 2
Identify the performance Obligations in the contract

Step 3
Determine the transaction Price

Step 4
Allocate the transaction price to the performance obligations in the contract

Step 5
Recognise revenue when (or as) the entity satisfies a performance obligation

> Remember the five steps as COPAR.

Note that, when applying the five-step approach, revenue will be recognised on one of two bases:

- **over a period of time** - likely to apply for the provision of services when there is simultaneous provision and consumption of a service, or

- **at a point in time** – likely to apply for the sales of goods when transfer of control can be determined at a specific point in time.

Step 1: Identify the contract

DEFINITION A **contract** is 'an agreement between two parties that creates rights and obligations' (IFRS 15).

An entity can only account for revenue from a contract if it meets the following criteria:

- the parties have approved the contract and each party's rights can be identified
- payment terms can be identified
- the contract has commercial substance
- it is probable that the selling entity will receive consideration.

Step 2: Identify the performance obligations

KEY POINT IFRS 15 says that the distinct performance obligations within a contract must be identified.

DEFINITION **Performance obligations** are promises to transfer distinct goods or services to a customer.

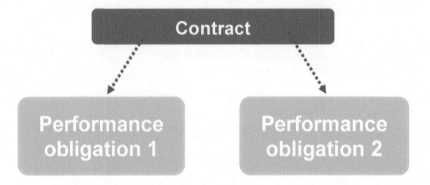

If a contract is made with a customer to sell a car with one year's free servicing, the sale of the car and the servicing are treated as separate performance obligations.

Step 3: Determine the transaction price

KEY POINT The transaction price is the consideration that the selling entity will be entitled to once it has fulfilled the performance obligations in the contract.

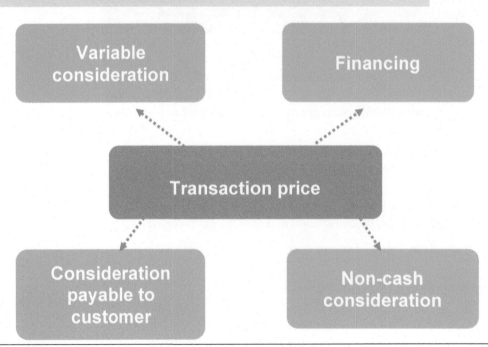

KEY POINT IFRS 15 says that if a contract includes variable consideration (e.g. a bonus or a penalty) then the entity must estimate the amount it expects to receive, but only include such value within the transaction price if the likelihood of payment is highly probable.

KEY POINT If there is a significant financing component, such as when the customer pays more than a year after receiving the goods or services, then the consideration receivable needs to be discounted to present value using the rate at which the customer borrows money.

KEY POINT Any non-cash consideration is measured at fair value.

KEY POINT If consideration is paid to a customer in exchange for a distinct good or service, then it should be accounted for as a separate purchase transaction.

Assuming that the consideration paid to a customer is not in exchange for a distinct good or service, an entity should account for it as a reduction in the transaction price.

Step 4: Allocate the transaction price

KEY POINT The total transaction price should be allocated to each performance obligation in proportion to standalone selling prices.

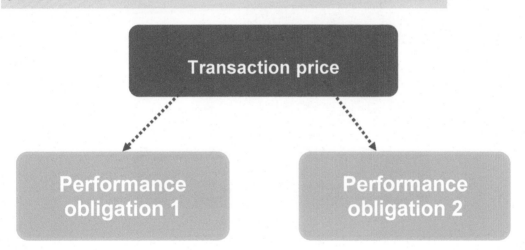

If a standalone selling price is not directly observable then it must be estimated.

Step 5: Recognise revenue

An entity must determine at contract inception whether it satisfies the performance obligation over time or at a point in time.

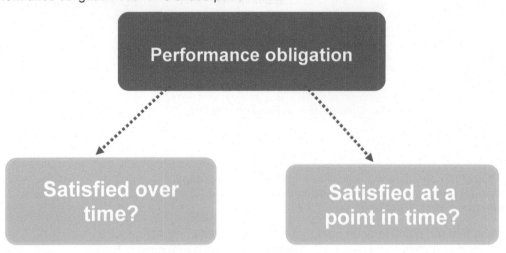

Performance obligations satisfied over time

IFRS 15 states that an entity only satisfies a performance obligation over time if **one** of the following criteria is met:

> The customer simultaneously receives and consumes the benefits from the entity's performance.

> The entity is creating or enhancing an asset controlled by the customer.

> The entity cannot use the asset 'for an alternative use' and the entity can demand payment for its performance to-date.

If a performance obligation is satisfied over time, then revenue is recognised based on the progress towards completion.

Progress towards completion may be measured using either an input method (based on costs incurred as a proportion of total expected cost) or an output method (based on value of work completed as a proportion of total contract price.

> The question will make clear whether the input method or output method should be used to measure the stage of completion.

Performance obligation satisfied at a point in time.

An entity controls an asset if it can direct its use and obtain its remaining benefits.

> Indicators that control ha passed to the customer include:
> - physical possession
> - transfer of significant risks and rewards
> - legal title
> - seller has right to payment.

12.2 STATEMENT OF FINANCIAL POSITION

LEARNING SUMMARY

After studying this section you should be able to:

•   explain and apply criteria for recognition of contract costs.

Contract costs

An entity must capitalise:

•   the costs of obtaining a contract

•   the costs of fulfilling a contract that do not fall within the scope of another standard (such as IAS 2 *Inventories*).

KEY POINT The capitalised costs are amortised to profit or loss as revenue is recognised.

Assets and liabilities

If the entity recognises revenue before it has received consideration then it should recognise either:

•   **a receivable** if the right to consideration is unconditional, or

•   **a contract asset.**

KEY POINT A contract liability is recognised if the entity receives consideration before the related revenue has been recognised.

1   Bettina, has prepared its draft financial statements for the year ended 30 September 20X4. It has included the following transactions in revenue at the stated amounts below.

   Which of these has been correctly included in revenue according to IFRS 15 *Revenue from Contracts with Customers*?

   A   Agency sales of $250,000 on which Bettina is entitled to a commission.

   B   Sale proceeds of $20,000 for motor vehicles which were no longer required by Bettina.

   C   Sales of $150,000 on 30 September 20X4. The amount invoiced to and received from the customer was $180,000, which includes $30,000 for ongoing servicing work to be done by Bettina over the next two years.

   D   Sales of $200,000 on 1 October 20X3 to an established customer which (with the agreement of Bettina) will be paid in full on 30 September 20X5. Bettina has a cost of capital of 10%.

2   Tanay entered into a contract to construct an asset for a customer on 1 January 20X4 which is expected to last 24 months. The agreed price for the contract is $5 million. At 30 September 20X4, the costs incurred on the contract were $1.6 million and the estimated remaining costs to complete were $2.4 million. On 20 September 20X4, Tanay received a payment from the customer of $1.8 million which was equal to the full amount billed. Tanay calculates the progress on the basis of amount billed compared to the contract price.

   What amount would be reported in Tanay's statement of financial position as at 30 September 20X4?

   $_____

3   **Which of the following is not one of the 5 steps for recognising revenue according to IFRS 15 *Revenue from Contracts with Customers*?**

   A   Identify the contract

   B   Assess the likelihood of economic benefits

   C   Determine the contract price

   D   Allocate the transaction price to the performance obligations in the contract.

13 Taxation

The following topics are covered in this chapter:
- Tax in the financial statements
- Deferred tax
- Deferred tax on asset revaluation

13.1 TAX IN THE FINANCIAL STATEMENTS

LEARNING SUMMARY

After studying this section you should be able to:
- account for current taxation in accordance with relevant accounting standards.

Tax expense

The tax expense in the financial statements is made up of two elements:

| Current tax | ····· | Tax payable to authorities in relation to current year activities, together with under or over provision from the previous years. |

| Deferred tax | ····· | An accounting adjustment aimed to match the tax effects of transactions to the relevant accounting period. |

KEY POINT The tax expense in the SPL = current tax +/- movement in deferred tax.

Accounting for current tax

| Dr Tax (SPL) | x | |
| Cr Tax payable (SFP) | | x |

> Remember that the current tax figure will only ever represent an estimate of tax based on current year profit which will be given to you in the question.

Do you understand?

1   Deferred tax is an application of the accruals concept.

    True or false.

1   True. Deferred tax matches the tax effects of transactions to the relevant accounting period which is an application of the accruals concept.

13.2 DEFERRED TAX

After studying this section you should be able to:

- explain the effect of taxable temporary differences on accounting and taxable profits

- compute and record deferred tax amounts in the financial statements.

KEY POINT The provision for deferred tax recognises the estimated future tax consequences of recognised transactions and events.

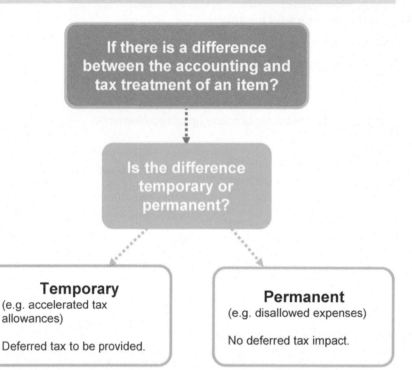

Calculating temporary differences

Deferred tax is calculated by comparing the carrying amount of an asset or liability to its tax base.

DEFINITION The **tax base** of an asset or liability is its value for tax purposes.

It is important to consider whether the carrying amount or the tax base is the larger figure:

Carrying amount > tax base (a taxable difference)	Carrying amount < tax base (a deductible difference)
Deferred tax liability	Deferred tax asset

Recognition

Measurement

When accounting for deferred tax, the entity accounts for the year-on-year movement in the deferred tax asset or liability. This is normally recorded in profit or loss:

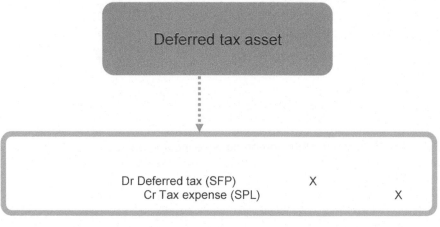

Deferred tax asset

Dr Deferred tax (SFP)	X
Cr Tax expense (SPL)	X

OR

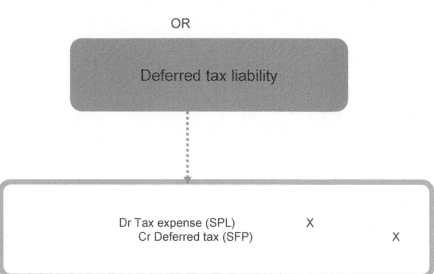

Deferred tax liability

Dr Tax expense (SPL)	X
Cr Deferred tax (SFP)	X

For F7 the temporary differences are likely to be limited to those arising on property, plant and equipment.

Remember it is only the movement in deferred tax which needs to be accounted for.

Do you understand?

1   A piece of machinery cost $500. Tax depreciation to date has amounted to $220 and depreciation charged in the financial statement to date is $100. The rate of income tax is 30%.

What is the deferred tax liability in relation to this asset?

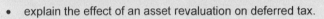

1    $36. Deferred tax liability = temporary difference × tax rate = ($220-$100) × 30% = $36.

13.3 DEFERRED TAX: ASSET REVALUATION

LEARNING SUMMARY

After studying this section you should be able to:

• explain the effect of an asset revaluation on deferred tax.

KEY POINT Deferred tax should be recognised on asset revaluations, even if there is no intention to sell the asset.

Revaluation gains are recorded in other comprehensive income and so any deferred tax arising on the revaluation must also be recorded as other comprehensive income.

Extract from the Statement of profit or loss and other comprehensive income for the year ended 31 December 20X9

Other comprehensive income:	
Revaluation of property	x
Transfer to deferred tax	x
	x

1   Bob Co's accounting records show the following:

Income tax payable for the year $60,000

Over provision in relation to the previous year $4,500

Opening provision for deferred tax $2,600

Closing provision for deferred tax $3,200

What is the income tax expense that will be shown in the Statement of Profit or Loss for the year?

A $54,900

B $67,700

C $65,100

D $56,100

2   Petra has the following balances included on its trial balance at 30 June 20X4:

Taxation $4,000 Credit

Deferred taxation $12,000 Credit

The balance on Taxation relates to an overprovision from 30 June 20X3.

At 30 June 20X4, the directors estimate that the provision necessary for taxation on current year profits is $15,000.

The carrying amount of Petra's non-current assets exceeds the tax written-down value by $30,000. The rate of tax is 30%.

What is the charge for taxation that will appear in the Statement of Profit or Loss for the year to 30 June 20X4?

A $23,000

B $28,000

C $8,000

D $12,000

14.1 BASIC EARNINGS PER SHARE (EPS)

LEARNING SUMMARY

After studying this section you should be able to:

- calculate the earnings per share (EPS) in accordance with relevant accounting standards, dealing with full market value issues, bonus issues and rights issues.

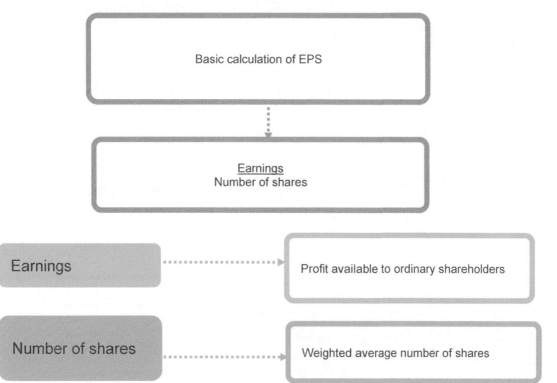

Basic calculation of EPS

$$\frac{\text{Earnings}}{\text{Number of shares}}$$

| Earnings | Profit available to ordinary shareholders |
| Number of shares | Weighted average number of shares |

Weighted average number of shares

The calculation of weighted average will depend of the type of share issue:

- Full market value issue – use weighted average table

- Bonus issue – assume bonus shares issued with original shares, so in issue for whole of current year

- Rights issue – use weighted average table (see below), with pre-issue shares adjusted for bonus element using rights issue bonus fraction. A four step process can be used.

Weighted average table pro-forma

	Number of shares	x Fraction of year held	x Bonus fraction (if applicable)	= Weighted average
b/f	X	X X/12	x X	X
Issue	X	X X/12		X
Total	X			
			Weighted average =	X

Step 1: Calculate the theoretical ex-rights price (TERP)

Start with the number of shares previously held by an individual at their market price. Then add in the number of new shares purchased at the rights price. You can then find the TERP by dividing the total value of these shares by the number held.

Step 2: Bonus fraction

$$\frac{\text{Market price before issue}}{\text{TERP}}$$

Step 3: Weighted average number of shares (WANS)

You would draw up a table (above) to calculate the weighted average number of shares. When doing this, the bonus fraction would be applied from the start of the year up to the date of the rights issue, but not afterwards.

Step 4: Earnings per share (EPS)

You can now calculate the EPS:

$$\frac{\text{PAT}}{\text{WANS}}$$

Example: rights issue

Ria had 6,000 ordinary shares in issue on 1 January 20X3.

On 1 April 20X3 Ria issued 1,500 shares in a 1 for 4 rights issue at a price of $2.50 when the market price per share was $4.

Ria's earnings for the year to 31 December 20X3 were $1,200.

Required:

Calculate Ria's earnings per share for the year to 31 December 20X3.

TERP calculation		No of shares	Price per share $	Total value $
	Holding	4	4.00	16.00
	Rights	1	2.50	2.50
		5		18.50

TERP = 18.50 ÷ 5 = $3.70

	No of shares	Fraction of year held	Rights issue bonus fraction	Weighted average
b/f	6,000	$\times 3/12$	$4/3.70$	1,622
Rights issue 1:4	1,500			
Total	7,500	$\times 9/12$		5,625
				7,247

Earnings per share = $1,200 ÷ 7,247 = 16.6¢

Example: bonus issue

Robert had 6,000 ordinary shares in issue on 1 January 20X3.

On 1 April 20X3 Robert issued 1,500 shares in a 1 for 4 bonus issue.

Robert's earnings for the year to 31 December 20X3 were $1,200.

Required:

Calculate Robert's earnings per share for the year to 31 December 20X3.

Bonus shares are deemed to have been in issue for full year.

	No of shares	Fraction of year held	Weighted average
b/f	6,000		
Bonus issue 1:4	1,500		
Total	7,500	$\times 12/12$	7,500

Earnings per share = 1,200 ÷ 7,500 = 16.0¢

14.2 DILUTED EARNINGS PER SHARE (DEPS)

LEARNING SUMMARY

After studying this section you should be able to:

* explain the relevance of the diluted earnings per share (DEPS) and calculate the DEPS involving convertible debt and share options (warrants).

Impact of diluting instruments

KEY POINT Equity share capital may change in the future owing to circumstances which exist now – known as dilution. The provision of a diluted EPS figure attempts to alert shareholders to the potential impact on EPS.

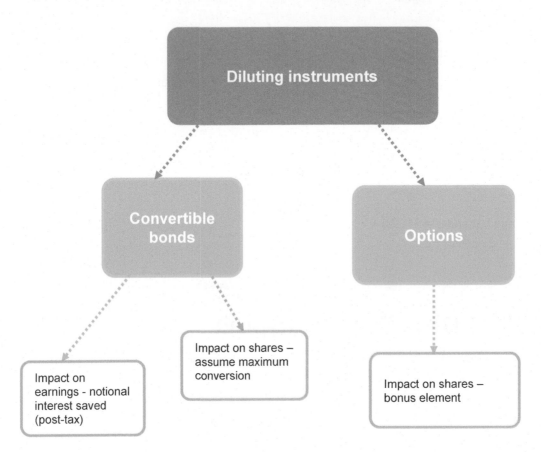

Purpose of DEPS

KEY POINT The purpose of DEPS is to show the potential impact on EPS of future share issues arising as a result of instruments in issue at the year-end.

Instruments to be considered are convertible debt (loan stock, bonds etc.) and share options.

Example: DEPS – convertibles

Ria had 6,000 ordinary shares in issue throughout the year to 31 December 20X3.

At that date Ria also had in issue $5,000 convertible loan stock with an effective rate of interest of 10%. Ria's rate of income tax is 30%.

The loan is convertible into ordinary shares on the basis of 60 shares per $100 loan.

Ria's earnings for the year to 31 December 20X3 were $1,200.

Required:

Calculate Ria's diluted earnings per share for the year to 31 December 20X3.

Basic number of shares		6,000
Conversion: $5,000 × $^{60}/_{\$100}$		3,000
		————
Adjusted number of shares		9,000
		————
	$	$
Basic earnings		1,200
Notional interest saved: $5,000 × 10%	500	
Tax @ 30%	(150)	
	————	350
		————
		1,550
		————

Diluted earnings per share = $1,550 ÷ 9,000 = 17.2¢

Example: DEPS – options

Ria had 6,000 ordinary shares in issue throughout the year to 31 December 20X3.

At that date Ria also had in issue 2,000 share options. These options are exercisable at $1.20 per ordinary share. The average fair value per ordinary share during the year was $1.50.

Ria's earnings for the year to 31 December 20X3 were $1,200.

Required:

Calculate Ria's diluted earnings per share for the year to 31 December 20X3.

Bonus element of options = $\dfrac{(1.50 - 1.20)}{1.50} \times 2,000 = 400$ shares

Diluted EPS = 1,200 ÷ (6,000 + 400) = 18.8¢

Exam style questions

The following scenario relates to questions 1–3

The profit after tax for Binford for the year ended 30 September 20X7 was $15 million. At 1 October 20X6 the company had in issue 36 million equity shares. On 1 January 20X7 Binford made a fully subscribed rights issue of one new share for every four shares held at a price of $2.80 each. The market price of the equity shares of Binford immediately before the issue was $3.80.

The profit after tax for Carmel for the year ended 30 September 20X7 was $15 million. At 1 October 20X6 the company had in issue 43.25 million equity shares and a $10 million convertible loan note which has an effective interest rate of 8%. The loan note will mature in 20X8 and will be redeemed at par or converted to equity shares on the basis of 25 shares for each $100 of loan note at the loan-note holders' option. The loan interest is tax deductible. Carmel's tax rate is 25%.

The profit after tax for Diota for the year ended 30 September 20X7 was $12 million. On 1 October 20X6 Diota had 34 million shares in issue. On 1 February 20X7 Diota made a market issue of 3 million shares at full price. On 1 July 20X7 Diota made a bonus issue of one new share for every five shares held.

1   **What is the basic earnings per share for Binford for the year ended 30 September 20X7?**

A $0.42

B $0.32

C $0.33

D $0.35

2   **What is the diluted earnings per share for Carmel for the year ended 30 September 20X7?**

A $0.34

B $0.35

C $0.36

D $0.33

3   **What is the basic earnings per share for Diota for the year ended 30 September 20X7?**

A $0.26

B $0.32

C $0.28

D $0.31

15

IAS 37 and IAS 10

The following topics are covered in this chapter:
- Provisions
- Specific situations
- Contingencies
- Events after the reporting period

15.1 PROVISIONS

LEARNING SUMMARY

After studying this section you should be able to:

- define a provision
- outline the criteria for recognising a provision
- account for a provision.

DEFINITION A **provision** is 'a liability of uncertain timing or amount' (IAS 37, para 10).

KEY POINT Given the uncertainty relating to provisions there is significant scope for accounting error, or even deliberate manipulation when accounting for provisions.

Recognition

To reduce the risk of error or manipulation, IAS 37 *Provisions, Contingent Liabilities and Contingent Assets* states three criteria for recognition of a provision.

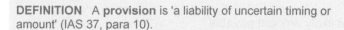

Criteria for recognising a provision:

There must be a present obligation (legal or constructive) that exists as the result of a past event.

There must be a probable transfer of economic benefits

There must be a reliable estimate of the potential cost.

Obligation

DEFINITION A **legal obligation** is an obligation that derives from:

- the terms of a contract,
- legislation, or
- other operation of law (IAS 37, para 10)

Note the three separate elements of a legal obligation.

DEFINITION A **constructive obligation** is an obligation that derives from an entity's actions where:

- by an established pattern of past practice, published policies, or a sufficiently specific current statement, the entity has indicated to other parties that it will accept certain responsibilities, and

- as a result, the entity has created a valid expectation on the part of those other parties that it will discharge those responsibilities (IAS 37, para 10)

Note the two separate elements of a constructive obligation.

Accounting for a provision

Upon recognition of a provision there must be an estimate of the potential cost of the uncertain event and immediate recognition in the financial statements. The accounting entries required are:

Dr	Expenses
Cr	Provision

KEY POINT The provision would be classified as a current or non-current liability in the statement of financial position depending on what is appropriate for the situation.

Measurement

KEY POINT Provisions should be measured at the best estimate of the expenditure required to settle the obligation as at the reporting date.

The best estimate of a provision will be:

- **for a single obligation:** the most likely amount payable

- **for a large population of items:** an expected value.

If the effect of the time value of money is material, then the provision should be discounted to present value.

15.2 SPECIFIC SITUATIONS

LEARNING SUMMARY

After studying this section you should be able to:

- identify and account for onerous contracts and environmental and similar provisions.

Future operating losses	No provision is recognised.

Onerous contracts	A provision should be recorded at the lower of: • the cost of fulfilling the contract • the cost of terminating the contract.

Restructuring	If there is an approved detailed plan and employees affected are aware of the plan then a provision should be recognised for the direct costs of the restructuring.

Environmental provisions	A provision is required if there is a legal or constructive obligation to carry out the work.

15.3 CONTINGENCIES

Contingent liability

DEFINITION A **contingent liability** is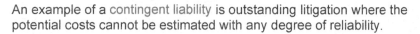

(a) 'a possible obligation that arises from past events and whose existence will be confirmed only by the occurrence or non-occurrence of one or more uncertain future events not wholly within the control of the entity; or

(b) a present obligation that arises from past events but is not recognised because:

  (i) it is not probable that an outflow of resources embodying economic benefits will be required to settle the obligation, or

  (ii) the amount of the obligation cannot be measured with sufficient reliability' (IAS 37, para 10).

An example of a contingent liability is outstanding litigation where the potential costs cannot be estimated with any degree of reliability.

Contingent asset

DEFINITION A **contingent asset** is 'a possible asset that arises from past events and whose existence will be confirmed only by the occurrence or non-occurrence of one or more uncertain future events not wholly within the control of the entity' (IAS 37, para 10).

An example of a contingent asset is a business making a claim for compensation from another party and the outcome of the claim is uncertain at the reporting date.

Accounting for contingent liabilities and contingent assets

Probability of occurrence	Contingent liabilities	Contingent assets
Virtually certain >95%	Provide	Recognise
Probable 51% – 95%	Provide	Disclosure note
Possible 5% – 50%	Disclosure note	Ignore
Remote <5%	Ignore	Ignore

15.4 EVENTS AFTER THE REPORTING PERIOD

LEARNING SUMMARY

After studying this section you should be able to:

* understand the accounting of events after the reporting period.

DEFINITION Events after the reporting period are 'those events, favourable and unfavourable, that occur between the end of the reporting period and the date when the financial statements are authorised for issue' (IAS 10, Para 3).

KEY POINT The purpose of IAS 10 is to define to what extent events that occur after the reporting period should be recognised in the financial statements.

Adjusting events — material events which provide additional evidence of conditions already in existence at the reporting date.

→ The financial statements should be adjusted to include the effect of such events.

Non-adjusting events — material events which do not concern conditions existing at the reporting date.

→ Impact going concern.

→ Adjust financial statements to present on the break-up basis.

→ Does not impact going concern.

→ Do not adjust the financial statements but disclose as a note if important to users' understanding.

Examples of adjusting events:

Discovery of errors or fraud that occurred during the reporting period

Resolution of an insurance claim or court case that confirms an obligation at the reporting date

Major customers going into liquidation

Examples of non-adjusting events

Fluctuations in tax/exchange rates

Issue of shares

Fire or flood after the reporting date

Do you understand?

1. Under what criteria is a provision recognised?

2. If the probability of occurrence of a contingent asset is virtually certain it can be disclosed within a note to the accounts.

   True or false?

3. Give two examples of non-adjusting events.

1. A provision should be recognised if (a) there is an obligation, (b) a transfer of economic benefits is probable, (c) a reliable estimate can be made.

2. False. If the probability of occurrence for a contingent asset is virtually certain it would be recognised in the accounts.

3. Examples of non-adjusting events are; fluctuations in tax/exchange rates, the issue of shares and fire or flood occurring after the reporting date.

1   Which of the following items require a provision in accordance with IAS 37 *Provisions, Contingent Liabilities and Contingent Assets*?

   (i)   An electronics retailer has a policy of providing refunds over and above the statutory requirement to do so. This policy is well publicised and customers have made use of this facility in the past.

   (ii) A customer has made a legal claim against an entity, claiming that faulty goods sold to them caused injury. The entity's lawyers have advised that the claim will possibly succeed and, if it does, compensation of $5,000 will be payable

   What is the charge to the Statement of Profit or Loss in respect of the above information?

   A   (i) only

   B   (ii) only

   C   (i) and (ii)

   D   Neither

2   **Which of the following statements about the requirements relating to IAS 37 *Provisions, Contingent Liabilities and Contingent Assets* are correct?**

   (i)   A contingent asset should be disclosed by note if an inflow of economic benefits is probable.

   (ii) No disclosure of a contingent liability is required if the possibility of a transfer of economic benefits arising is remote.

   (iii) Contingent assets must not be recognised in financial statements unless an inflow of economic benefits is virtually certain to arise.

   A   All three statements are correct.

   B   (i) and (ii) only

   C   (i) and (iii) only

   D   (ii) and (iii) only

3   Using the requirements set out in IAS 10 *Events after the Reporting Period,* which of the following would be classified as an adjusting event after the reporting period in financial statements ended 31 March 20X4 that were approved by the directors on 31 August 20X4?

A   A reorganisation of the enterprise, proposed by a director on 31 January 20X4 and agreed by the Board on 10 July 20X4.

B   A strike by the workforce which started on 1 May 20X4 and stopped all production for 10 weeks before being settled.

C   The receipt of cash from a claim on an insurance policy for damage caused by a fire in a warehouse on 1 January 20X4. The claim was made in January 20X4 and the amount of the claim had not been recognised at 31 March 20X4 as it was uncertain that any money would be paid. The insurance enterprise settled with a payment of $1.5 million on 1 June 20X4.

D   The enterprise had made large export sales to the USA during the year. The year-end receivables included $2 million for amounts outstanding that were due to be paid in US dollars between 1 April 20X4 and 1 July 20X4. By the time these amounts were received, the exchange rate had moved in favour.

16

Principles of consolidated financial statements

The following topics are covered in this chapter:

- Concept of group accounts
- Alternative sources of power
- Uniform accounting policies

16.1 CONCEPT OF GROUP ACCOUNTS

LEARNING SUMMARY

After studying this section you should be able to:

- define and explain terms relevant to group accounting.

Control

> **DEFINITION** A **group** exists where one entity, the parent (referred to as 'the investor'), has control over another entity, the subsidiary (referred to as 'the investee').

IFRS 10 specifies three criteria that must be present for control to be established:

Power over the investee, which is normally exercised through the majority of voting rights (i.e. owning more than 50% of the equity shares).

Exposure or rights to variable returns from involvement (e.g. a dividend).

The ability to use power over the investee to affect the amount of investor returns. This is regarded as a crucial determinant in deciding whether or not control is exercised (IFRS 10, para 7).

> **DEFINITION** A **parent** is an entity that controls one or more entities (IFRS 10, Appendix A).

> **DEFINITION** A **subsidiary** is an entity that is controlled by another entity (IFRS 10. Appendix A).

> **DEFINITION** A **non-controlling interest** is 'an equity in a subsidiary not attributable, directly or indirectly, to a parent' (IFRS 10, Appendix A).

> Remember definitions as they may be tested in the objective test part of the examination.

Single entity concept

In treating the two companies as a single entity it becomes necessary to remove any intra-group transactions or balances in order to present consolidated financial statements.

16.2 ALTERNATIVE SOURCES OF POWER

LEARNING SUMMARY

After studying this section you should be able to:

- explain alternative sources when control may be achieved.

Other sources of power

Contractual arrangements between the parent and other parties.

Holding a minority shareholding but with the remaining equity held by a large, dispersed and unconnected group of shareholders.

Potential voting rights (e.g. share options) resulting in control being gained at a specific date.

In a long form question the most likely source of power will be the ownership by the parent of the majority of voting shares within the subsidiarv.

16.3 UNIFORM ACCOUNTING POLICIES

LEARNING SUMMARY

After studying this section you should be able to:

- explain how to deal with the need for uniform accounting policies.

Where the subsidiary has policies that differ from that of the group, adjustments will be necessary as part of the consolidation process to ensure consistency.

Do you understand?

1   What percentage ownership would be required for holding the majority of voting rights?

2   What is the definition of a group?

1   Owning more than 50% of the equity shares.
2   A group exists where one entity (referred to as the 'investor'), has control over another entity, the subsidiary (referred to as the 'investee').

1   **Which one of the following definitions is not included within the definition of control per IFRS 10?**

    A   Having power over the investee

    B   Having exposure, or rights, to variable returns from its investment with the investee

    C   Having the majority of shares in the investee

    D   Having the ability to use its power over the investee to affect the amount of the investor's return

2   **Which of the following would normally indicate that one entity has control over the activities of another?**

    A   Ownership of some equity shares in another entity

    B   Ownership of up to twenty per cent of the equity shares of another entity

    C   Ownership of over fifty per cent of the equity shares of another entity

    D   Ownership of between twenty per cent and fifty per cent of the equity shares of another entity

17 Consolidated statement of financial position

The following topics are covered in this chapter:
- Mechanics of consolidation
- Fair values
- Intra-group trading

17.1 MECHANICS OF CONSOLIDATION

LEARNING SUMMARY

After studying this section you should be able to:
- prepare a consolidated statement of financial position for a simple group.

Standard workings

There are five standard workings when producing a consolidated statement of financial position.

(W1) Group structure

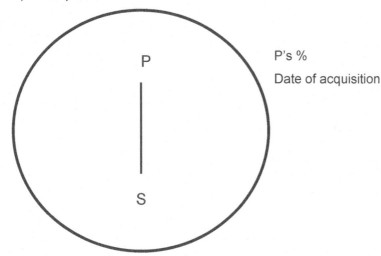

P's %

Date of acquisition

(W2) Net assets of subsidiary

	Acquisition	Reporting date	Post-acquisition
	$m	$m	$m
Share capital	X	X	
Retained earnings	X	X	X
Other components of equity	X	X	X
Fair value adjustments (FVA)	X	X	X
Post-acquisition depreciation of FVA	–	(X)	(X)
PURP adjustment (if S is seller)	–	(X)	(X)
(covered below)			
	X	X	X
	to W3		to W4/W5

Remember the difference between reserves at reporting date and the acquisition date is split between the group (W5) and the non-controlling interest (W4).

(W3) Goodwill

	$m
Fair value of consideration	X
Non-controlling interest at acquisition (see below)	X
Subsidiary's net assets at acquisition (W2)	(X)
Goodwill at acquisition	X
Impairment	(X)
Goodwill at reporting date	X

The non-controlling interest at acquisition can either be measured at:

- fair value (either given in question or sufficient detail to calculate)
- its proportionate share of the fair value of the subsidiary's net assets at the acquisition date.

KEY POINT Negative goodwill (a gain on bargain purchase) is credited to the statement of profit or loss, and therefore added to retained earnings (W5).

(W4) Non-controlling interest

	$m
NCI at acquisition (as per W3)	X
NCI% × S's post acquisition reserves (W2)	X
NCI% × goodwill impairment (**FV method only**)	(X)
NCI at reporting date	X

(W5) Consolidated reserves

	Retained earnings	Other components
	$m	$m
100% P's reserves	X	X
P's % of S's post-acquisition reserves (W2)	X	X
Goodwill impairment	(X)	–
Gain on bargain purchase (W3)	X	–
PURP adjustment (if P was seller)	(X)	–
Reserves at reporting date	X	X

> Be careful when dealing with goodwill impairment in retained earnings.
>
> Deduct P's % if the NCI was valued at fair value.
>
> Deduct in full if the NCI was valued using the proportional method.

17.2 FAIR VALUES

Fair values of consideration

When calculating goodwill in (W3), purchase consideration is measured at fair value.

Method of payment	Measurement	Journal
Cash at acquisition	Cash paid	Dr Cost of investment (W3) Cr Cash
Deferred cash	Present value (PV)	Dr Cost of investment (W3) Cr Liability
Shares at acquisition	Fair value at acquisition	Dr Cost of investment (W3) Cr Share capital Cr Share premium
Deferred shares	Fair value at acquisition	Dr Cost of investment (W3) Cr Other components of equity
Contingent consideration	Fair value	Dr Cost of investment (W3) Cr Liability/Equity

> The question will provide the figure for the fair value of contingent consideration or provide enough information to calculate it.

KEY POINT Professional fees are expensed to the profit or loss.

Fair value of subsidiary's net assets

Where assets and liabilities are not carried at their fair value, adjustments will therefore be necessary. These will be adjusted on (W2) **and** on the statement of financial position.

> Take care to complete both sides of the adjustment.

Typical fair value adjustments could include:

- property, plant and equipment

    Adjustments to depreciating assets will need to reflect any post-acquisition depreciation in the reporting date column of (W2).

- inventory

    Remember to amend adjustments to inventory in the reporting date column to allow for any inventory sold in the post-acquisition period.

- intangible assets not recognised by the subsidiary

    This type of asset (e.g. an internally generated brand), although not recognised by the subsidiary will need to be added to the subsidiary's assets as a consolidation adjustment, reflecting any post-acquisition amortisation as necessary.

- contingent liabilities

    Again these will not be recognised by the subsidiary and will need to be deducted from (W2) and inserted on the consolidated statement of financial position, reflecting any post-acquisition adjustment as necessary.

17.3 INTRA-GROUP TRADING

LEARNING SUMMARY

After studying this section you should be able to:

- account for the effects of intra-group balances.

KEY POINT All intra-group balances must be removed.

Trading balances

- Remove both the asset and liability.

- Where asset and liability are not equal, adjust for cash and/or goods in transit before removing the balanced asset and liability.

A goods in transit adjustment will require a subsequent PURP adjustment (see below).

PURP adjustments – inventory

KEY POINT At the reporting date if a group company holds inventory that has been purchased from another group company, the profit included within that inventory is removed by means of a Provision for UnRealised Profit (PURP) adjustment.

The impact is to reduce the value of inventory to its group cost and reduce the retained earnings of the selling company. If the parent is the seller reflect the reduction in (W5), and where the subsidiary is the seller reflect the reduction in the reporting date column in (W2).

PURP adjustments – non-current assets

KEY POINT At the reporting date if a group company holds a non-current asset that has been purchased from another group company, the profit included within that non-current asset is removed by means of a Provision for UnRealised Profit (PURP) adjustment.

The impact is to reduce the value of the asset to its group cost.

For PURPs on non-current assets there are two adjustments to retained earnings. The seller's retained earnings are reduced by the total original profit on the asset, while the purchaser's retained earnings are increased by the value of the excess depreciation charged.

Do you understand?

1   How is the fair value of deferred cash measured?

2   How is negative goodwill treated in the consolidated statement of financial position?

4   What is the purpose of making fair value adjustments?

1   Deferred cash is measured at present value.

2   Negative goodwill is added to group retained earnings through (W5).

3   The need to account on a fair value basis reflects the statement of financial position often valuing items (mainly non-current assets) at their historic cost less depreciation. This may mean the carrying value of those assets is significantly different to their current market values.

1 At 1 January 20X8 Bina acquired 80% of the share capital of Maya for $100,000. At that date the share capital of Maya consisted of 50,000 ordinary shares of $1 each and its reserves were $30,000. At 31 December 20X9 the reserves of Bina and Maya were as follows:

Bina $400,000

Maya $50,000

In the consolidated statement of financial position of Bina and its subsidiary Maya at 31 December 20X9, what amount should appear for group reserves?

A $400,000

B $438,000

C $416,000

D $404,000

2 At 1 January 20X6 Drake acquired 60% of the share capital of Calvin for $35,000. At that date the share capital of Calvin consisted of 20,000 ordinary shares of $1 each and its reserves were $10,000. At 31 December 20X9 the reserves of Drake and Calvin were as follows:

Drake $40,000

Calvin $15,000

At the date of acquisition the fair value of the non-controlling interest was valued at $25,000.

In the consolidated statement of financial position of Drake and its subsidiary Calvin at 31 December 20X9, what amount should appear for non-controlling interest?

A $25,000

B $27,000

C $28,000

D $31,000

3   The statements of financial position for Picanto and Sienna as at
     31 December 20X6 are presented below:

Assets	Picanto	Sienna
Non-current assets	$	$
Property, plant and equipment	300,000	225,000
Investments	400,000	–
Current assets		
Inventories	80,000	75,000
Trade and other receivables	60,000	140,000
Cash and cash equivalents	10,000	25,000
Total assets	850,000	465,000
Equity and liabilities		
Equity		
Share capital	80,000	60,000
Share premium	20,000	10,000
Retained earnings	295,000	250,000
Non-current liabilities		
Loans	300,000	85,000
Current liabilities		
Trade and other payables	155,000	60,000
Total equity and liabilities	850,000	465,000

The following notes are relevant to the preparation of the consolidated
financial statements:

(i)   Picanto acquired 80% of the ordinary shares of Sienna for
       $400,000 on 1 January 20X2. At the acquisition date, the
       retained earnings of Sienna were $150,000. The fair value of
       the non-controlling interest in Sienna at the date of acquisition
       was $80,000.

(ii)   At the date of acquisition, the fair values of the net assets of
       Sienna approximated their carrying amounts, with the
       exception of a plot of land owned by Sienna. This land was
       held in the financial statements of Sienna at its cost of
       $150,000 but was estimated to have a fair value of $180,000.
       This land was still owned by Sienna at 31 December 20X6.

(iii) During the year, Picanto sold goods to Sienna for $50,000
       making a gross profit margin on the sale of 25%. Two fifths of
       these goods are still included in the inventories of Sienna at
       31 December 20X6.

Required:

**Prepare the consolidated statement of financial position for the
Picanto group as at 31 December 20X6.**

Consolidated statement of profit or loss

18.1 MECHANICS OF CONSOLIDATION

LEARNING SUMMARY

After studying this section you should be able to:

- prepare a consolidated statement of profit or loss and other comprehensive income
- account for the effects of intra-group trading.

KEY POINT The consolidated statement of profit or loss follows the same basic principles as the consolidated statement of financial position.

The basic method of preparing a consolidated statement of profit or loss

1	Add together the income, expenses and any other comprehensive income of the parent and the subsidiary on a line-by-line basis.
2	Eliminate intra-group items, such as trading and dividends received from the subsidiary.
3	Make consolidation adjustments: • PURP (increase cost of sales) • Fair value depreciation (usually cost of sales but check the question) • Impairment (administration costs/operating expenses)
4	Calculate the profits attributable to the non-controlling interests (NCI). After profit for the year, show the split of profit between amounts attributable to the parent's shareholders and the non-controlling interest (to reflect ownership).

A consolidated statement of profit or loss doesn't require standard workings like a consolidated statement of financial position. Many of the adjustments can be made on the face of the statement of profit or loss.

Non-controlling interest (NCI)

	$
Subsidiary's profit after tax[1]	X
PURP (when the sub is the seller only)	(X)
Fair value depreciation	(X)
Impairment (fair value method only)	(X)
Adjusted subsidiary profit	X
x NCI % = profit attributable to NCI	X

Work out the NCI profit first and then the balancing figure belongs to the parent company.

Note [1] Where acquisition takes place part-way through the current year, the subsidiary's profit after tax will represent the post-acquisition element.

18.2 MID-YEAR ACQUISITIONS

Procedure

- When combining subsidiary performance, only include post-acquisition revenue and expenses.

- Assume revenue and expenses accrue evenly unless told otherwise.

- Where dividends have been received from the subsidiary in the post-acquisition period these should be removed from group investment income. Dividends in the pre-acquisition period will be incorporated within the calculation of net assets at acquisition.

- Remove any intra-group items, such as trading (revenue and cost of sales), taking care to only exclude the post-acquisition element.

- Make consolidation adjustments:

    - PURP, period end adjustment so recognise in full

    - Fair value depreciation, post-acquisition only, so time-apportion

    - Impairment, period end adjustment so recognise in full.

- Show split of profits and total comprehensive income between parent and NCI, taking care with NCI to only include post-acquisition elements.

Do you understand?

1 Robin acquires 80% of the share capital of Sparrow on 1 August 20X6 and is preparing its group financial statements for the year ended 31 December 20X6.

How will Sparrow's results be included in the group statement of profit or loss?

2 A goodwill impairment will not impact the non-controlling interest's share of profit if the non-controlling interest is measured at fair value.

True or false?

3 Are intra-group sales added or deducted from the group sales revenue figure?

---

1 All of Sparrow's revenue and expenses will be time-apportioned from the date of acquisition to the date of consolidation to reflect the period for which these were controlled by Robin.

2 False. The goodwill impairment will reduce the non-controlling interest's share of profit by the non-controlling interest's share of the goodwill impairment.

3 Intra-group sales are deducted from the group sales revenue figure.

1   Entity X acquired sixty per cent of the issued equity shares of entity Z on 1 October 20X3. During the year ended 31 December 20X3, X and Z had sales revenue of $2 million and $1.5 million respectively. During the post-acquisition period, X made sales to Z of $0.1 million.

What is the group sales revenue figure for the year ended 31 December 20X3?

A $2.275 million

B $2.375 million

C $3.4 million

D $3.5 million

2   On 1 July 20X5 George acquired sixty per cent of the equity shares of Bungle. For the year ended 31 December 20X5, George made a profit after tax of $600,000 and Bungle had a profit after tax of $400,000. During the post-acquisition period, George sold goods to Bungle which included a profit element of $20,000. At the year-end, one quarter of the goods sold by George to Bungle remained within the inventory of Bungle.

What was the non-controlling interest share of the group profit after tax for the year ended 31 December 20X5?

A $75,000

B $80,000

C $120,000

D $160,000

3   The following statements of profit or loss relate to Pecan and its subsidiary Sultana for the year ended 31 December 20X6:

	Pecan	Sultana
	$000	$000
Revenue	200,000	100,000
Cost of sales	(110,000)	(50,000)
Gross profit	90,000	50,000
Distribution costs	(20,000)	(10,000)
Administrative expenses	(40,000)	(20,000)
Operating profit	30,000	20,000
Investment income from Sultana	7,500	
Profit before tax	37,500	20,000
Taxation	(10,500)	(6,000)
Profit for the year	27,000	14,000

The following notes are relevant to the preparation of the consolidated financial statements:

(i)   Pecan acquired three million of the equity shares of Sultana on 30 June 20X6 when Sultana had a total of four million equity shares in issue. Pecan paid a total of $25 million to acquire the shares.

(ii)   At 30 June 20X6, the retained earnings of Sultana were $20 million and the carrying amounts of the net assets of Sultana approximated to their fair values.

(iii)   It is group accounting policy to account for non-controlling interest at its fair value. At the date of acquisition, the fair value of the non-controlling interest in Sultana was $7 million.

(iv)   During the post-acquisition period, Sultana sold goods to Pecan. The goods originally cost $10 million and they were sold to Pecan at a mark-up of 25%. At 31 December 20X6, Pecan still had 40% of these goods within its inventory.

Required:

(a)   Calculate goodwill arising on acquisition of Sultana by Pecan.

(b)   Prepare the consolidated statement of profit or loss for the Pecan group for the year ended 31 December 20X6.

19 Associates

The following topics are covered in this chapter:
- Definitions and accounting
- Consolidated statement of financial position
- Inter-company trading and fair values
- Consolidated statement of profit or loss

19.1 DEFINITIONS AND ACCOUNTING

LEARNING SUMMARY

After studying this section you should be able to:

- define an associate
- explain the use of equity accounting.

DEFINITION An **associate** is defined as 'an entity over which the investor has significant influence' (IAS 28, para 3).

DEFINITION **Significant influence** is 'the power to participate in the financial and operating policy decisions of the investee but is not control or joint control over those policies' (IAS 28, para 3).

KEY POINT An investor is presumed to have significant influence over another entity when it has a shareholding in that other entity between 20% and 50%.

The associate is accounted for using equity accounting.

Equity accounting

DEFINITION **Equity accounting** is a method of accounting where the investment is initially recorded at cost and adjusted thereafter for the post-acquisition change in the investor's share of net assets of the associate.

The effect of this is summarised for both the consolidated statement of financial position and consolidated statement of profit or loss:

Equity accounting in the consolidated statement of financial position	Equity accounting in the consolidated statement of profit or loss
A single 'investments in associates' line within non-current assets which includes the group share of the assets and liabilities of any associate.	A single 'share of profit of associates' line which includes the group share of any associate's profit after tax.

> Under equity accounting you do not consolidate the equity on a line-by-line basis.

19.2 CONSOLIDATED STATEMENT OF FINANCIAL POSITION

LEARNING SUMMARY

After studying this section you should be able to:

* prepare a consolidated statement of financial position for a simple group, including an associate.

Impact on standard consolidated statement of financial position workings

(W1) Group structure

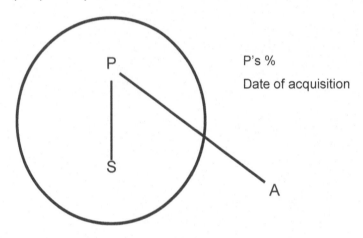

P's %

Date of acquisition

(W5) Consolidated reserves

	Retained earnings	Other components
	$m	$m
100% P's reserves	X	X
P's % of S's post-acquisition reserves (W2)	X	X
P's % of A's post acquisition reserves	X	X
Goodwill impairment	(X)	-
Impairment of investment in associate	X	-
PURP adjustment (if P **or** A was seller)	(X)	-
Reserves at reporting date	X	X

(W6) Investment in associate

	$m
Cost of investment	X
P's % of A's post-acquisition reserves	X
Less:	
Impairment of investment in associate	(X)
PURP adjustment	(X)
	X

19.3 INTER-COMPANY TRADING AND FAIR VALUES

LEARNING SUMMARY

After studying this section you should be able to:

* explain the effect of inter-company trading with an associate

* explain the effect of fair values of the associate's assets on consolidation.

Trading with the associate

* **DO NOT** eliminate balances between the associate and group companies, e.g. receivables and payables.

* **DO NOT** eliminate trading between the associate and group companies, e.g. revenue and cost of sales

* Remove dividends received from associate from the statement of profit or loss

* **PURP** required where goods sold by or to associate are unsold at the year-end

Provision for unrealised profit (PURP)

* Calculated as for subsidiary but only recognise parent's share.

* In statement of financial position

    – Reduce group retained earnings (W5)

    – Reduce investment in associate (W6).

* In statement of profit or loss reduce the share of associate profit (see below).

Fair values

Where the fair values of the associate's net assets at acquisition are different to their carrying amount the net assets should be adjusted as for a subsidiary. The effects of this would include adjustments to post-acquisition earnings for fair value depreciation adjustments or similar items.

19.4 CONSOLIDATED STATEMENT OF PROFIT OR LOSS

Single line in statement of profit or loss

The share of associate profit figure in the statement of profit or loss is made up as follows:

	$m
Parent share of associate profit for the year	X
Impairment for the year	(X)
PURP adjustment (calculated as above)	(X)
Share of associate profit per consolidated statement of profit or loss	X

Do you understand?

1. What is equity accounting?
2. What percentage ownership is considered to be a 'significant influence'?
3. How are inter-company balances with an associate treated under equity accounting?

1. Equity accounting is a method of accounting where the investment is initially recorded at cost and adjusted thereafter for the post-acquisition change in the investor's share of net assets of the associate.
2. An investor is presumed to have significant influence over another entity when it has a shareholding in that other entity between 20% and 50%.
3. Inter-company balances between the associate and group companies are not eliminated.

1   On 1 April 2009 Petr purchased 80% of the equity shares in Simone. On the same date Petr acquired 40% of the 40 million equity shares in Adil paying $2 per share.

The statement of profit or loss for the year ended 30 September 2009 are:

	Petr	Simone	Adil
	$000	$000	$000
Revenue	210,000	150,000	50,000
Cost of sales	(126,000)	(100,000)	(40,000)
Gross profit	84,000	50,000	10,000
Distribution costs	(11,200)	(7,000)	(5,000)
Administrative expenses	(18,300)	(9,000)	(11,000)
Investment income (interest and dividends)	9,500		
Finance costs	(1,800)	(3,000)	Nil
Profit (loss) before tax	62,200	31,000	(6,000)
Income tax (expense) relief	(15,000)	(10,000)	1,000
Profit (loss) for the year	47,200	21,000	(5,000)

The following information is relevant:

(i)   The fair values of the net assets of Simone at the date of acquisition were equal to their carrying amounts with the exception of an item of plant which had a carrying amount of $12 million and a fair value of $17 million. This plant had a remaining life of five years (straight-line depreciation) at the date of acquisition of Simone. All depreciation is charged to cost of sales.

The fair value of the plant has not been reflected in Simone's financial statements.

No fair value adjustments were required on the acquisition of the investment in Adil.

(ii)   Immediately after its acquisition of Simone, Petr invested $50 million in an 8% loan note from Simone. All interest accruing to 30 September 2009 has been accounted for by both companies. Simone also has other loans in issue at 30 September 2009.

(iii) Simone paid a dividend of $8 million during the year.

(iv)   After the acquisition, Petr sold goods to Simone for $15 million on which Petr made a gross profit of 20%. Simone had one third of these goods still in its inventory at 30 September 2009. Petr also sold goods to Adil for $6 million, making the same margin. Adil had half of these goods still in inventory at 30 September 2009.

(v)   The non-controlling interest in Simone is to be valued at its (full) fair value at the date of acquisition.

(vi) The goodwill of Simone has been impaired by $2 million at 30 September 2009. Due to its losses, the value of Petr's investment in Adil has been impaired by $3 million at 30 September 2009.

(vii) All items in the above statement of profit or loss are deemed to accrue evenly over the year unless otherwise indicated.

Required:

(a) **Calculate the carrying amount of the investment in Adil to be included within the consolidated statement of financial position as at 30 September 2009.**

(b) **Prepare the consolidated statement of profit or loss for the Petr Group for the year ended 30 September 2009.**

20 Group disposals

The following topics are covered in this chapter:

- Disposal of a subsidiary
- Treatment in the parent financial statements
- Treatment in the consolidated financial statements

20.1 DISPOSAL OF A SUBSIDIARY

LEARNING SUMMARY

After studying this section you should be able to:

- explain the effect of the disposal of a parent's investment in a subsidiary.

The disposal of a subsidiary needs to be reflected in:

- parent individual financial statements; and
- group financial statements.

Take care as the calculations of profit for each are very different.

20.2 TREATMENT IN THE PARENT FINANCIAL STATEMENTS

LEARNING SUMMARY

After studying this section you should be able to:

- illustrate the effect of the disposal of a parent's investment in a subsidiary in the parent's individual financial statements.

Parent's Statement of Profit or Loss

	$
Sale proceeds	X
Carrying amount of investment	(X)
Profit/(loss) in Parent Statement of Profit or Loss	X

Reporting

KEY POINT The profit or loss is shown separately as an exceptional item on the face of the Statement of Profit or Loss below profit from operations.

Tax is calculated on the parent's profit NOT group profit.

20.3 TREATMENT IN THE CONSOLIDATED FINANCIAL STATEMENTS

LEARNING SUMMARY

After studying this section you should be able to:

- illustrate the effect of the disposal of a parent's investment in a subsidiary in the group financial statements.

> You will only be tested on a full disposal of a subsidiary in F7 i.e. all of the shares in the subsidiary are sold.

Impact on consolidated financial statements

Statement of profit or loss

- Subsidiary results consolidated up to the date of disposal
- Profit/loss on disposal
- Alternative: treat as a discontinued operation (covered in Chapter 5).

Statement of financial position

- Subsidiary not consolidated
- Profit/loss on disposal included within retained earnings.

Consolidated Statement of Profit or Loss

		$
Sale proceeds		X
Net assets of subsidiary at disposal	X	
Unimpaired goodwill at disposal	X	
Non-controlling interest at disposal	(X)	
		(X)
Profit/(loss) in consolidated SPL		X

Calculation of values at disposal

You may be required to calculate one or more of the values in the above calculation.

Net assets

If fair value adjustments are necessary, it may be helpful to use a standard Working 2 with columns for acquisition, disposal and post-acquisition.

If necessary to calculate the assets due to a mid-year disposal:

	$
Net assets b/f	X
Profit/(loss) to date of disposal	X
Dividends paid prior to disposal	(X)
Net assets at disposal date	X

Goodwill

For calculation of goodwill use a standalone Working 3, remembering to deduct any impairment.

	$
Cost of investment	X
Fair value of NCI	X
Net assets at acquisition	(X)
Goodwill at acquisition	X
Impairment	(X)
Goodwill at disposal	X

Non-controlling interest (NCI)

For calculation of NCI use a standard Statement of Financial Position Working 4 to the date of disposal.

	$
Value at acquisition	X
Impairment	(X)
Post-acquisition profit	X
	X

Do you understand?

1   The profit or loss on disposal of a subsidiary should be recorded in Other Comprehensive Income.

   True or false?

2   The disposal of a subsidiary has no impact on the parent's individual financial statements.

   True or false?

3   The non-controlling interest at the date of disposal must be removed from the consolidated statement of financial position.

   True or false?

1   False. The gain or loss on disposal should be recorded in the statement of profit or loss, not other comprehensive income.

2   False. The disposal of a subsidiary will still affect the parent's financial statements, as the subsidiary will be recorded as an investment in the parent's books.

3   True. All elements of the subsidiary must be removed from the consolidated statement of financial position.

1   Identify whether the following statements are true or false.

	True	False
If a subsidiary is disposed of on the last day of the reporting period then its assets and liabilities must still be included in the consolidated statement of financial position		
The gain or loss arising on the disposal of a subsidiary in the consolidated financial statements is recorded in other comprehensive income		

2   The Cake group has a reporting date of 31 December 20X3. On 30 September 20X3, the group disposed of its 80% holding in the ordinary shares of Sugar for $10 million in cash. It has been deemed that the disposal of Sugar constitutes a discontinued operation. The following information relates to Sugar:

	$m
Goodwill at disposal	2
Net assets at disposal	9
Non-controlling interest at disposal	3

What should be recorded as the 'profit (or loss) on disposal in the consolidated statement of profit or loss for the year ended 31 December 20X3?

A   Loss of $2 million

B   Profit of $2 million

C   Profit of $4 million

D   Loss of $4 million

3   Hail purchased 80% of the ordinary shares of Rain for $4 million many years ago and holds the investment in its individual statement of financial position at cost. On 30 September 20X3, Hail disposed of its shares in Rain for $10 million in cash.

What is the profit arising on the disposal of the shares that will be reported in Hail's individual statement of profit or loss for the year ended 30 September 20X3?

$_____m

21 Interpretation of financial statements

The following topics are covered in this chapter:

- Interpreting financial information
- Ratio analysis
- Profitability ratios
- Liquidity and efficiency ratios
- Financial position ratios
- Investor ratios
- Limitations of ratio analysis

21.1 INTERPRETING FINANCIAL INFORMATION

LEARNING SUMMARY

After studying this section you should be able to:

- understand what interpretation of financial information aims to achieve.

It is important that users of financial statements can interpret the financial statements to be able to draw out valid conclusions. Ratio analysis is widely used for this purpose.

Interpretation involves comparisons of:

- prior years

- forecasts

- competitor performance.

Users can compare sales and expense figures, asset and liability balances and cash flows to perform this analysis.

> Note that ratio analysis is about both understanding financial data and what it means as well as enabling comparisons.

KEY POINT Ratio analysis is a tool to assist understanding and comparison.

21.2 RATIO ANALYSIS

LEARNING SUMMARY

After studying this section you should be able to:

- outline what ratio analysis is and the classification of ratios.

KEY POINT Ratios use simple calculations based upon the interactions within sets of data.

When analysing financial data and using ratios to do so, consider the following questions:

- What does the ratio mean?

- What does a change in the ratio mean?

- What is the norm or expectation?

- What are the limitations of the ratio?

> Scenarios may ask for a calculation or demonstration of understanding of the ratios and performance area.

21.3 PROFITABILITY RATIOS

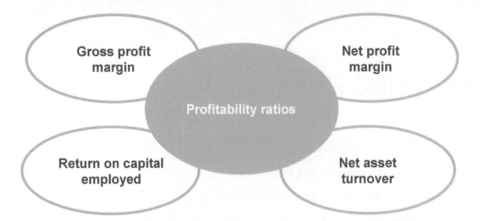

Gross profit margin

DEFINITION   On a unit basis the **gross profit** represents the
difference between the unit sales price and the direct cost per
unit.

The margin works this out on an average basis across all sales for the year.

$$\frac{\text{Gross profit}}{\text{Sales revenue}} \times 100$$

Changes may be due to:
- selling prices
- product mix
- purchase costs
- production costs
- inventory valuations.

Operating profit margin

DEFINITION   The **operating profit margin** is an expansion
of the gross profit margin. It includes all of the items that
come after gross profit but before finance charges and
taxation, such as distribution and administration costs in the
statement of profit or loss.

$$\frac{\text{Operating profit}}{\text{Sales revenue}} \times 100$$

If the gross profit margin has remained
static but the operating profit margin has
changed, consider the following possible
causes:
- changes in employment patterns (recruitment, redundancy etc.)
- changes to depreciation due to large acquisitions or disposals
- significant write-offs of irrecoverable debt
- changes in rental agreements
- significant investments in advertising
- rapidly changing fuel costs.

Return on capital employed (ROCE)

DEFINITION ROCE measures how much operating profit is generated for every $1 capital invested in the business.

$$\frac{\text{Operating profit}}{\text{Capital employed}} \times 100$$

KEY POINT Capital employed can be measured in either of the two following ways:

- equity plus interest-bearing finance, i.e. non-current loans plus share capital and reserves or

- total assets less current liabilities.

Either method will provide the same end answer to calculate capital employed.

Net asset turnover

DEFINITION The **net asset turnover** measures management's efficiency in generating revenue from the net assets at its disposal.

The net asset turnover is similar to ROCE but instead we measure the amount of sales revenue generated for every $1 capital invested in the business.

$$\frac{\text{Sales revenue}}{\text{Capital employed (net assets)}}$$

Relationship between ratios

ROCE can be subdivided into operating profit margin and asset turnover:

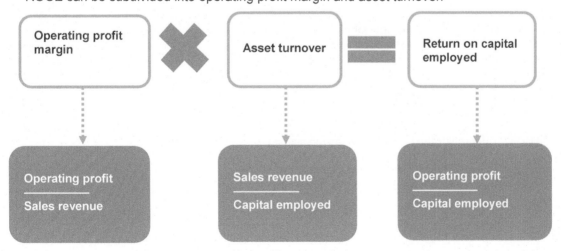

21.4 LIQUIDITY AND EFFICIENCY RATIOS

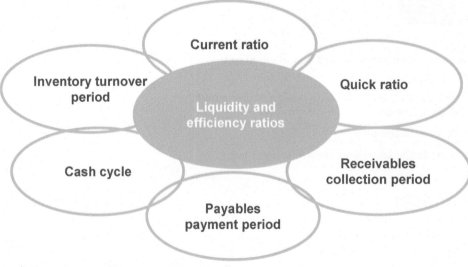

Current ratio

> **DEFINITION** The **current ratio** measures the adequacy of current assets to meet liabilities as they fall due.

$$\frac{\text{Current assets}}{\text{Current liabilities}} : 1$$

An increasingly high current ratio may appear safe but may be due to:
- high levels of inventory and receivables – indicating inventory that cannot be sold and poor credit control over receivables.
- high cash levels – indicating a loss of investment opportunities.

KEY POINT Traditionally, a current ratio of 2:1 or higher was regarded as appropriate for most businesses to maintain creditworthiness. However, more recently a figure of 1.5:1 is regarded as the norm.

Consideration must be given to the nature of the business. For example supermarkets tend to have few trade receivables, high levels of trade payables and tight cash control to fund investment

Quick ratio (acid test)

> **DEFINITION** The **quick ratio** is also known as the acid test ratio because by eliminating inventory from current assets it provides the acid test of whether the company has sufficient liquid resources (receivables and cash) to settle its liabilities.

$$\frac{(\text{Current assets} - \text{inventory})}{\text{Current liabilities}} : 1$$

When interpreting the quick ratio, care should be taken over the status of the bank overdraft. A business with a low quick ratio may have no issue paying amounts due if sufficient overall overdraft facilities are available.

Inventory turnover period

$$\frac{\text{Inventory}}{\text{Cost of sales}} \times 365 \text{ days}$$

An increasingly number of inventory days may indicate:
- holding onto inventory for longer
- buying bulk to take advantage of trade discounts
- reducing the risk of 'stockouts'
- preparation for an expected increase in orders.

Consequences of an increased inventory turnover period are the costs of storing, handling and insuring inventory levels will also increase. There is also an increased risk of inventory damage and obsolescence.

An alternative calculation is to calculate inventory turnover as a number of time per annum:

$$\frac{\text{Cost of sales}}{\text{Inventory}}$$

- A high turnover indicates a low level of inventory held in comparison to overall sales. Costs of holding inventory are reduced.
- A low inventory turnover indicates a high level of inventory is held in comparison to overall sales levels. Costs of holding inventory are increased.

Receivables collection period

$$\frac{\text{Trade receivables}}{\text{Credit sales}} \times 365 \text{ days}$$

Increasing receivables collection days may indicate a lack of proper credit control but can be due to:
- A significant new customer being allowed different (longer) terms.
- A deliberate policy to increase allowable credit terms to attract more trade.

The receivables days' ratio can be distorted by a number of factors:

- using year-end figures as opposed to average receivables,

- using factoring of accounts receivables figures which results in very low trade receivables,

- sales on unusually long credit terms to a select few customers which is out of the norm.

Payables collection period

DEFINITION The **payables collection period** is, on average, the credit period taken by the company from its suppliers.

The payables collection period is calculated as follows:

$$\frac{\text{Trade payables}}{\text{Credit purchases}} \times 365 \text{ days}$$

Increasing payables payment days may indicate:
- the company is unable to pay more quickly because of liquidity problems.
A long credit period may be good as it represents a source of free finance.

KEY POINT If the credit period is long the company may develop a poor reputation as a slow payer. Existing suppliers may decide to discontinue supplies and new suppliers may not be prepared to offer credit. Also the business may be losing out on worthwhile cash discounts for prompt payment.

Working capital cycle

The working capital cycle can be used to determine how many days cash is tied up as follows:

Inventory turnover period + receivables collection period – payables payment period.

KEY POINT Ideally, businesses would like to have cash tied up in working capital for the minimum number of days possible.

A shorter working capital cycle indicates a higher level of efficiency.

21.5 FINANCIAL POSITION RATIOS

LEARNING SUMMARY

After studying this section you should be able to:

- calculate and understand the meaning of financial position ratios.

Gearing

When assessing the financial position of a business the main focus is its stability and exposure to risk. This is typically assessed by considering the gearing.

DEFINITION Gearing is the way the business is structure and financed.

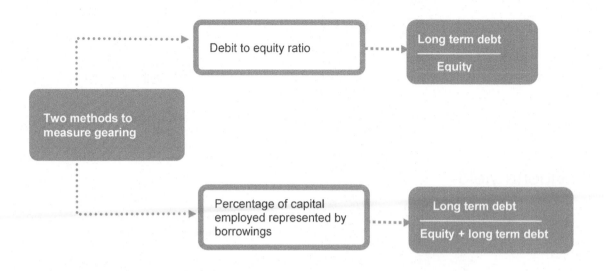

Two methods to measure gearing ·····> Debit to equity ratio ····>

$$\frac{\text{Long term debt}}{\text{Equity}}$$

Two methods to measure gearing ·····> Percentage of capital employed represented by borrowings ····>

$$\frac{\text{Long term debt}}{\text{Equity} + \text{long term debt}}$$

KEY POINT Long term debt includes non-current loan and redeemable preference share liabilities. Equity includes share capital (and premium) balances plus reserves (revaluation reserve, retained earnings).

Interest cover

DEFINITION Interest cover indicates the ability of a company to pay interest out of profits generated.

Interest cover is calculated as follows:

$$\frac{\text{Profit before interest and tax}}{\text{Interest payable}}$$

·····> Low levels of interest cover (less than two is deemed unsatisfactory) indicates:
- shareholders' dividends are at risk as profits are eaten up by interest payments
- the business may have difficulty financing its debts if its profits fall further.

21.6 INVESTOR RATIOS

LEARNING SUMMARY

After studying this section you should be able to:

- calculate and understand the meaning of investor ratios.

Earnings per share

$$\frac{\text{Profit available to ordinary shareholders}}{\text{Number of ordinary shares}}$$

·····> Measures the amount of profit a company makes per share issued in the company.

Price/Earnings (P/E) ratio

$$\frac{\text{Current share price}}{\text{Latest EPS}}$$

Represents a measure of market confidence in a company's capacity for growth.

A high P/E ratio suggests that high growth is expected.

Dividend yield

$$\frac{\text{Dividend per share}}{\text{Current share price}}$$

Measures the potential return on investment for prospective investors.

Can be compared to yields available on alternative investments.

Dividend cover

$$\frac{\text{Profit after tax}}{\text{Dividends}}$$

Similar to interest cover, indicates how many times current dividend could be paid from current profit level.

High cover indicates that current dividend level is able to be maintained.

Do you understand?

1   What are the two methods to measure gearing?

2   The trade receivables days for ABC Ltd have increased – this could be due to an increase in credit terms as an incentive to attract customers.

    True or false?

3   Why does the quick ratio exclude inventory from current assets?

4   What does net asset turnover measure?

---

1   The two methods to measure gearing are 1) debt to equity ratio and 2) percentage of capital employed represented by borrowings.
2   True.
3   Inventory is excluded from the quick ratio as it is considered to potentially be a slow-moving asset so emphasis is concentrated on having sufficient liquid assets to cover current liabilities.
4   Net asset turnover measures management's efficiency in generating revenue from the net assets at its disposal.

21.7 LIMITATIONS OF RATIO ANALYSIS

LEARNING SUMMARY

After studying this section you should be able to:

• state the limitations of ratio analysis.

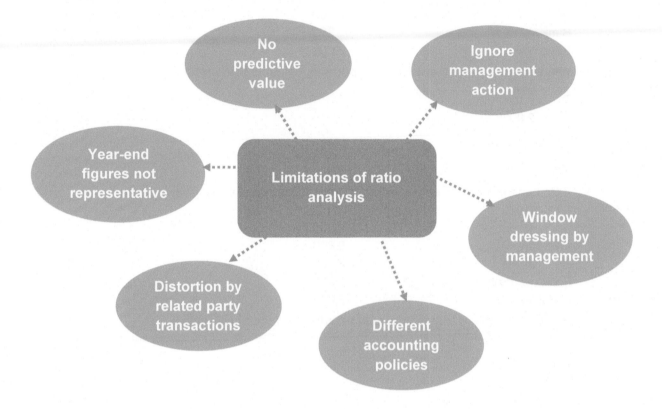

1   Z Co had the following details extracted from its statement of financial position:

	$000
Inventory	3,800
Receivables	2,000
Bank overdraft	200
Payables	2,000

What was the current ratio based upon the available information?

A   1.72:1

B   2.90:1

C   2.64:1

D   3.00:1

2   Z Co had the following details extracted from its statement of financial position:

	$000
Inventory	3,800
Receivables	2,000
Bank overdraft	200
Payables	2,000

Based upon the available information, what was the quick (acid test) ratio of Z Co?

A   2.63 : 1

B   0.9 : 1

C   29.0 : 1

D   1 : 1

3   **Which one of the following is likely to reduce the trade payables payment period?**

A   Offering credit customers a significant discount for prompt payment within seven days of receipt of invoice

B   Paying trade suppliers within seven days of receipt of invoice to obtain a discount

C   Buying proportionately more goods on a cash basis, rather than on a credit basis

D   Buying an increasing volume of credit purchases during an accounting period

4   On 1 July 20X5, X Co raised $5 million from an issue of ordinary shares. X Co then immediately used this cash to repay a loan of $5 million, which was not due for repayment until 30 June 20X9.

What impact did this have upon the debt/equity ratio?

A   It is not possible to determine the impact on the debt/equity ratio as there is insufficient information available

B   The debt/equity ratio increased

C   The debt/equity ratio decreased

D   There will be no change to the debt/equity ratio

22 Statement of cash flows

The following topics are covered in this chapter:
- The purpose and format of a statement of cash flows
- Cash flows from operating activities
- Cash flows from investing activities
- Cash flows from financing activities
- Cash flow information

22.1 THE PURPOSE AND FORMAT OF A STATEMENT OF CASH FLOWS

LEARNING SUMMARY

After studying this section you should be able to:

- differentiate between profit and cash flow
- understand the purpose of preparing a statement of cash flows
- outline the format of a statement of cash flows.

Profit and cash

Whilst a business entity might be profitable this does not mean it will be able to survive. To survive a business needs cash to be able to pay its debts. If it cannot pay its debts, the business would become insolvent and could not continue to operate.

KEY POINT Profit is not the same as cash flow.

Why does profit not equal the change in cash and bank balances?

Profit is calculated on an accruals basis. Bank and cash balances change when monies are received and paid out.

→ The accruals basis means income and expense are recognised when earned or incurred not when cash is received or paid.

The calculation of profit includes some items that do not affect cash at all or affect it differently.

→ Examples:
- Depreciation is deducted from profit but involves no movement in cash.
- The profit or loss on disposal of a non-current asset is included in profit for the year, but it is the proceeds of sale that affect the cash and bank balances.
- Any change in the allowance for receivables will affect profit for the year, but will not affect cash flows.

Bank and cash balances are affected by some items that do not affect profit.

→ Examples:
- Purchase of non-current assets (only depreciation affects profit)
- Raising additional capital
- Repayment of loans.

IAS 7 *Statement of Cash Flows* requires companies to prepare a statement of cash flows as part of their annual financial statements. The statement of cash flows must be presented using standard headings.

The format of a statement of cash flows

Statement of cash flows	
	$
Cash flows from operating activities	
Cash generated from operations	X
Interest paid	(X)
Taxation paid	(X)
Net cash from operating activities	X
Cash flows from investing activities	
Purchase of non-current assets	(X)
Proceeds from the sale of non-current assets	X
Interest received	X
Dividends received	X
Net cash from investing activities	X
Cash flows from financing activities	
Issue of shares	X
Loan repaid	(X)
Loan issued	X
Dividends paid	(X)
Net cash from financing activities	X
Net increase/(decrease) in cash and cash equivalents	X(/X)
Cash and cash equivalents b/fwd	X
Cash and cash equivalents c/fwd	X

Change in c
balances fro
principal
revenue
producing
activities.

Change in c
balances fro
gains or los
from
investments

Change in c
balances fro
activities rai
and repayin
finance.

22.2 CASH FLOWS FROM OPERATING ACTIVITIES

LEARNING SUMMARY

After studying this section you should be able to:

- calculate the cash flow from operating activities using the indirect and direct method

- calculate the figures needed for the statement of cash flows including cash flows from operating activities.

There are two methods of presenting cash flows from operations:

- **Direct method** – based upon cash flow information extracted directly from the accounting records. This method discloses information that would otherwise remain confidential and so most business entities do not use the direct method.

> You need to learn both methods of presentation and be able to apply either method in the examination if required.

Cash flows from operating activities	
	$
Cash receipts from customers	X
Cash payments to suppliers	(X)
Cash payments to employees	(X)
Cash payments for expenses	(X)
Cash generated from operations	X
Interest paid	(X)
Tax paid	(X)
Net cash flow from operations	(X)/X

- **Indirect method** – relies upon information that is disclosed in or calculated from the financial statements. The starting point is normally profit before tax, which is adjusted to remove any non-cash items or accruals-based figures included in the statement of profit or loss.

Depreciation	Added back to profit before tax as it is a non-cash expense.
Profit or loss on disposal of non-current assets	Non-cash income or expense so deducted or added back – cash proceeds on disposal are classified as an investing activity.
Investment income and finance costs	Finance costs are added back and investment income is deducted as they are not part of cash generated from operations.
Movement in inventory	Inventory represents purchases made in one period, which will be charged against profit in another period. An increase in inventory is deducted from profit before tax as it is a cash outflow to pay for additional inventory. A decrease in inventory is added to profit before tax as it is a cash inflow from disposing of inventory
Movement in receivables	Receivables represent revenue recognised in one period, with the cash being received in next. A decrease in receivables is added to profit before tax (cash inflow) as more cash has been collected from receivables. An increase in trade receivables is deducted from profit before tax.
Movement in payables	Payables represent purchases made in one period, which will be paid in the next. An increase means the business has had the use or benefit of the entity but not paid for them – cash reserves are preserved. A decrease in payables means more payables have been paid - deducted from profit before tax as a cash outflow.

. Cash flows from operating activities	
	$
Profit before taxation	X
Depreciation/amortisation charge	X
(Profit)/loss on disposal of non-current assets	(X)/X
Investment income	(X)
Finance costs	X
Operating profit before working capital changes	X
(Increase)/decrease in inventories	(X)/X
(Increase)/decrease in trade and other receivables	(X)/X
Increase/(decrease) in trade and other payables	X/(X)
Cash generated from operations	X
Interest paid	(X)
Tax paid	(X)
Net cash flow from operating activities	X/(X)

KEY POINT The cash flow should be calculated by reference to the charge to profits for the item (shown in the statement of profit or loss) and any opening or closing payable balance (shown on the statement of financial position).

A ledger account approach or a list approach can be used to help with calculations.

Interest/tax payable			
	$		$
		Bal b/fwd (SFP)	X
Cash paid (β)	X	Expense for the year (SPL)	X
Bal c/fwd (SFP)	X		
	—		—
	X		X
	—		—

22.3 CASH FLOWS FROM INVESTING ACTIVITIES

LEARNING SUMMARY

After studying this section you should be able to:

- calculate the figures needed for the statement of cash flows including cash flows from investing activities.

Investing activities cash inflows may include:

- interest received

- dividends received

- proceeds of sale of non-current assets.

Investing activities cash outflows may include:

- purchase of property, plant and equipment.

Interest and dividends received

The calculation of interest received and dividends received should take account of both the income shown in the statement of profit or loss and any relevant receivables balance from the opening and closing statements of financial position.

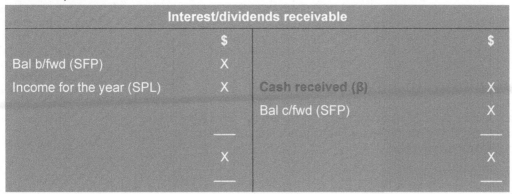

Interest/dividends receivable			
	$		$
Bal b/fwd (SFP)	X		
Income for the year (SPL)	X	Cash received (β)	X
		Bal c/fwd (SFP)	X
	___		___
	X		X
	___		___

Proceeds from the sale of non-current assets

Proceeds from the sale of non-current assets can be calculated if the carrying amount of the non-current asset being disposed is known and whether a profit or loss has been made on disposal.

- If a profit has been made on disposal, the proceeds can be calculated by adding the profit to the carrying amount of the disposed asset.

- If a loss has been made on disposal, the proceeds can be calculated by deducting the loss from the carrying amount of the disposed asset.

Purchase of property, plant and equipment

The purchase of property, plant and equipment and resulting cash outflow can be calculated with a ledger account approach.

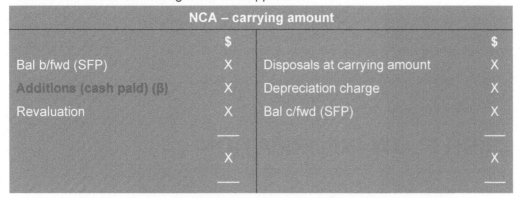

NCA – carrying amount			
	$		$
Bal b/fwd (SFP)	X	Disposals at carrying amount	X
Additions (cash paid) (β)	X	Depreciation charge	X
Revaluation	X	Bal c/fwd (SFP)	X
	___		___
	X		X
	___		___

22.4 CASH FLOWS FROM FINANCING ACTIVITIES

LEARNING SUMMARY

After studying this section you should be able to:

- calculate the figures needed for the statement of cash flows including cash flows from financing activities.

Financing activities cash inflows may include:

- proceeds of the issue of shares

- proceeds of receipt of loans/debentures.

Financing activities cash outflows may include:

- repayment of loans/debentures
- dividends paid
- interest paid.

> **KEY POINT** IAS 7 permits interest paid to be classified as a cash outflow within either operating activities or as a financing activity.

Ensure that the cash outflow for interest paid in the year is classified either within operating activities or within financing activities and not included twice within the statement of cash flows.

Proceeds from the issue of shares

Proceeds from the issue of shares can be calculated by comparing the amounts included in the statement of financial position brought forward and carried forward on two accounts:

- share capital
- share premium.

> **KEY POINT** If there is a bonus issue made in the year; this will not result in a cash inflow.

Proceeds of receipt of loans or repayment of loans

The cash flows in relation to a loan can be calculated by comparing the amounts included in the statement of financial position brought forward and carried forward.

A fall in the amount outstanding indicates that all or part of the loan has been repaid in the year (a cash outflow). An increase indicates that there has been a further loan received in the year (a cash inflow).

Dividends paid

As dividends paid are effectively paid out of retained earnings, it is usually necessary to reconcile the opening and closing balances on retained earnings to identify any dividend paid in the year as a balancing figure.

> **KEY POINT** IAS 7 permits dividends paid to be classified as either an operating cash flow or as a financing cash flow. It is more usual to classify dividends paid as a financing cash flow.

22.5 CASH FLOW INFORMATION

LEARNING SUMMARY

After studying this section you should be able to:

- explain the advantages and limitations of cash flow statements
- interpret a cash flow statement.

Advantages of cash flow statements

- Helps users make judgements on future cash flows.
- Indicates the relationship between profit and cash generated.
- Helps users check accuracy of previous assessments.
- Difficult to manipulate.

Limitations of cash flow statements

- Based on historical information, so no predictive quality.
- Small scope for manipulation, e.g. delay payments at year-end.
- No indication of profitability, necessary for long-term survival.

Interpretation of cash flow statements

When reviewing a cash flow statement focus on the following areas:

- Cash generated from operations – indicates sustainability
- Capital expenditure
- Sources of finance
- Net cash flow.

Do you understand?

1 If a profit has been made on disposal, the proceeds can be calculated by deducting the profit from the carrying amount of the disposed asset.

   True or false?

2 IAS 7 Statement of cash flows requires companies to prepare a statement of cash flows as part of their annual financial statements. Activities are split into three categories – what are those categories?

3 Name a cash inflow from a financing activity.

4 Explain both the direct and indirect method to present cash flows from operating activities.

1 False: if a profit has been made on disposal, the proceeds can be calculated by adding the profit to the carrying amount of the disposed asset.

2 Activities can be classified as; operating, investing and financing activities.

3 A cash inflow from a financing activity; proceeds of the issue of shares or proceeds of receipt of loans/debentures.

4 **Direct method** – based upon cash flow information extracted directly from the accounting records. This method discloses information that would otherwise remain confidential and so most business entities do not use the direct method.

   Indirect method – relies upon information that is disclosed in or calculated from the financial statements. The starting point is normally profit before tax, which is adjusted to remove any non-cash items or accruals-based figures included in the statement of profit or loss.

1 **State whether each of the following statements is true or false.**

A A statement of cash flows prepared using the direct method produces a different figure for investing activities in comparison with that produced if the indirect method is used.

B A bonus issue of shares does not feature in a statement of cash flows.

C The amortisation charge for the year on intangible assets will appear as an item under 'Cash flows from operating activities' in a statement of cash flows.

D Loss on the sale of a non-current asset will appear as an item under 'Cash flows from investing activities' in a statement of cash flows.

2 Extracts from the financial statements of Deuce Co showed balances as follows:

	20X9	20X8
$1 Share capital	300,000	120,000
Share premium	260,000	100,000

A bonus issue of 1 share for every 12 held at the 20X8 year-end occurred during the year and loan notes of $300,000 were issued at par. Interest of $12,000 was paid during the year.

What is the net cash inflow from financing activities?

A $480,000

B $605,000

C $617,000

D $640,000

3 A business has made a profit of $8,000 but its bank balance has fallen by $5,000.

Which one of the following statements could be a possible explanation for this situation?

A Depreciation charge of $3,000 and an increase in inventories of $10,000

B Depreciation charge of $6,000 and the repayment of a loan of $7,000

C Depreciation charge of $12,000 and the purchase of new non-current assets for $25,000

D The disposal of a non-current asset for $13,000 less than its carrying amount

4 A statement of cash flows prepared in accordance with the indirect method reconciles profit before tax to cash generated from operations.

Which of the following lists of items consists only of items that would be ADDED to profit before tax?

A Decrease in inventory, depreciation charge, profit on sale of non-current assets

B Increase in payables, decrease in receivables, profit on sale of non-current assets

C Loss on sale of non-current assets, depreciation charge, increase in receivables

D Decrease in receivables, increase in payables, loss on sale of non-current assets

5 The following financial statements and supporting information relate to Philomena, a limited liability entity:

Statement of profit or loss and other comprehensive income for the year ended 30 June 20X5

	$000
Revenue	113,250
Cost of sales	(77,500)
Gross profit	35,750
Distribution costs	(3,000)
Administration expenses	(1,000)
Interest payable	(750)
Profit before tax	31,000
Income tax expense	(6,000)
Profit for the year	25,000
Other comprehensive income:	
Revaluation of property, plant and equipment	2,000
Total comprehensive income for the year	27,000

Statement of financial position at 30 June 20X5

	20X5	20X4
	$000	$000
ASSETS		
Non-current assets		
Property, plant and equipment	110,000	93,000
Current assets		
Inventories	36,000	30,000
Trade receivables	40,000	35,000
Cash and equivalents	Nil	10,000
Total assets	186,000	168,000

EQUITY AND LIABILITIES

Equity share capital	20,000	15,000
Share premium	8,000	3,000
Revaluation reserve	10,000	8,000
Retained earnings	96,000	85,000
Total equity	134,000	111,000
Non-current liabilities		
Bank loan	7,000	17,000
Current liabilities		
Trade payables	36,500	30,000
Income tax	6,500	10,000
Bank overdraft	2,000	Nil
Total equity and liabilities	186,000	168,000

Notes:

The following information is relevant to the financial statements of Philomena:

(i)   During the year ended 30 June 20X5, Philomena disposed of several items of plant and equipment for sale proceeds of $8,000,000. The loss on disposal of $2,000,000 is included within cost of sales. The depreciation charge for the year was $15,000,000.

(ii)   Philomena estimated that the income tax liability arising on the profit for the year ended 30 June 20X5 was $6,500,000.

Required:

Based upon the available information, prepare a statement of cash flows using the indirect method for Philomena for the year ended 30 June 20X5 in accordance with the requirements of IAS 7 *Statement of Cash Flows*.

CHAPTER 1

1

> **KEY POINT** Remember that, although it may be tempting to do a lot of work on your calculator, you should also include your workings as part of your submitted answers so that the marker can see what you have done. If you are not completely correct with your workings, you will be given credit for appropriate method, but the marker can only do this is they can see and understand what you have done.

Statement of profit or loss and other comprehensive income for the year ended 30 June 20X1

	$000
Revenue	100,926
Cost of sales	(67,051)
Gross profit	33,875
Distribution costs	(7,826)
Administrative expenses	(11,761)
Profit from operations	14,288
Finance costs	(1,000)
Profit before taxation	13,288
Income tax expense	(2,700)
Profit for the year	10,588
Other comprehensive income for the year	
Surplus on revaluation of land	14,000
Total comprehensive income for the year	24,588

Refer to W1 for cost of sales

Refer to W2 for distribution costs

Refer to W3 for admin expenses

Refer to W4 for finance costs

Refer to W5 for revaluation

Statement of financial position as at 30 June 20X1

	$000
Non-current assets	
Property, plant and equipment	119,500
Current assets	
Inventories	9,420
Trade and other receivables	20,800
Cash and cash equivalents	2,213
Total assets	151,933

Refer to W6 for PPE

Refer to W7 for receivables

Equity	
Share capital	50,000
Share premium	25,000
Retained earnings	20,508
Revaluation reserve ($10,000 + $14,000)	24,000
Non-current liabilities	
5% bank loan	20,000
Current liabilities	
Trade and other payables	9,725
Tax payable	2,700
	_____
Equity and liabilities	151,933
	_____

Refer to W5 for revaluation

Refer to W9 for payables

Refer to W8 for retained earnings

CHAPTER 2

1   C

2   IAS 40 Investment properties defines an investment property as land or a buildings held to earn rentals, or for capital appreciation or both, rather than for use in the entity or for sale by the entity in the ordinary course of business.

3   D and E

CHAPTER 3

1   A

The finance was only available after the year end. Therefore the criteria of recognising an asset were not met, as the resources were not available to complete the project.

Even though the brand is internally generated in the subsidiary's accounts, it can be recognised at fair value for the group. Item C can be recognised as a purchased intangible and item D meets the criteria for being capitalised has development costs.

2   D

Item A cannot be capitalised because it does not meet all the criteria, i.e. it is not viable.

Item B is research and cannot be capitalised.

Item C cannot be capitalised because it does not meet all the criteria, i.e. making a loss.

3   B, C

Key staff cannot be capitalised as firstly they are not controlled by an entity. Secondly, the value that one member of key staff contributes to an entity cannot be measured reliably.

CHAPTER 4

1   **B**

A is incorrect as the recoverable amount is the higher of the value in use and fair value less costs to sell. C is wrong as it describes fair value, not value in use. D is wrong as impairment losses can be taken to the revaluation surplus if one exists for that asset.

2   **A**

The plant had a carrying amount of $240,000 on 1 October 20X4. The accident that may have caused impairment occurred on 1 April 20X5 and an impairment test would be done at this date.

The depreciation on the plant from 1 October 20X4 to 1 April 20X5 would be $40,000 (640,000 × 12.5% × 6/12) giving a carrying amount of $200,000 at the date of impairment.

3   **B**

The recoverable amount of the plant is the higher of its value in use of $150,000 or its fair value less costs to sell. If Desert trades in the plant it would receive $180,000 by way of a part exchange, but this is conditional on buying new plant which Desert is reluctant to do.

A more realistic amount of the fair value of the plant is its current disposal value of only $20,000. Thus the recoverable amount would be its value in use of $150,000.

4   **B**

First, the brand must be completely written off.

Writing this off would give a remaining carrying amount of $20 million ($12 million land and $8 million plant) meaning that $5 million must be allocated across the other assets.

Therefore the $5 million should be allocated across the land and the plant on a pro-rata basis according to their carrying amounts.

Impairment to plant = 8,000/20,000 × 5,000 = $2,000. Therefore carrying amount is $6 million.

5   **A**

Annual impairment reviews are required for intangible assets with an indefinite life, intangible assets not yet ready for use, and goodwill.

Other items should have impairment reviews when indications of impairment exist.

CHAPTER 5

1   **A**

Assets held for sale should be held at the lower of carrying value and fair value less costs to sell. Therefore the asset should be held at $750.

Item B is just the fair value. Item C is the fair value plus the costs to sell, which is incorrect. Item D is the carrying value.

2   **C**

A sale has to be expected within 12 months, not one month. The others are all criteria which must be met to classify an asset as held for sale.

	Shown on the face of the statement of profit or loss	Not shown
Revenue		X
Gross profit		X
Profit after tax	X	

One line should be shown regarding profit from discontinued operations. This line is the profit after tax from the discontinued operation, with a full breakdown of the amount in the notes to the accounts.

4

	Discontinued operation Yes/No
Sector X	No
Sector Y	Yes

Although Sector X is the only operation of Total Co in Country A, it is not a separate major line of geographical operations, as it only contributes 0.5% of Total Co revenue. Therefore Total Co would not report this as a discontinued operation.

Sector Y is a separate major line of business operations, as it contributes a significant amount of Total Co revenue, and produces a different item from the other parts of Total Co. Therefore, Total Co would report Sector Y as a discontinued operation.

CHAPTER 6

1   C

2   D

All of the remaining answers include only part of the full definition of an asset.

3   C

4   **B and D**

The remaining answers are fundamental qualitative characteristics.

CHAPTER 7

1   B

2   A

3   A

In times of rising prices, asset values will be understated, as historical cost will not be a true representation of the asset values. Additionally, the real purchase cost of replacement items will not be incorporated, meaning that profits are overstated

CHAPTER 8

1

	Change in accounting policy	Change in accounting estimate
Classifying commission earned as revenue in the statement of profit or loss, having previously classified it as other operating income	X	
Revising the remaining useful life of a depreciable asset		X

2   **$55,800**

	Cost	Recoverable amount (Net Realisable Value)	Lower of cost and recoverable amount
Item 1	$24,000	See note 1	$24,000
Item 2	$33,600	$31,800 (note 2)	$31,800
			_____
			$55,800
			_____

Notes:

(1)   The recoverable amount is not known, but it must be above cost because the contract is expected to produce a high profit margin. The subsequent fall in the cost price to $20,000 is irrelevant for the inventory valuation.

(2)   The recoverable amount is $36,000 minus 50% of $8,400.

3   **D**

Biological assets should be revalued to fair value less point of sale costs at the year end, with the gain or loss being taken to the statement of profit or loss.

CHAPTER 9

1   **C**

The lease grants the lessee the beneficial rights of asset use, meaning that a right-of-use asset and lease liability are recorded.

2   **A**

Leased assets are exempt from capitalisation where the lease period is for 12 months or less, or the assets are low-value assets

3   **$306,250**

The plant would be capitalised at $350,000, equal to the lease liability plus the initial payment. This would then be depreciated over the four year lease term, giving depreciation of $87,500 a year.

As Fino only entered into the lease halfway through the year, this would give depreciation of $43,750. Therefore the carrying amount would be $350,000 less $43,750, which is $306,250.

4 **A**

	$
Present value of total lease payments	350,000
Less initial lease rental	(100,000)
Initial lease liability	250,000
Interest to 30 September 20X7 (6 months at 10%)	12,500

5

	Increase	**Decrease**
Return on Capital Employed		✓
Gearing	✓	
Interest cover		✓

Recognition of the lease liability would cause debt liabilities and finance costs to increase. This means that the capital employed would be higher, therefore decreasing return on capital employed. Gearing would increase due to the increased debt. Interest cover would decrease due to the higher level of finance costs.

CHAPTER 10

1 **B**

The loan notes should initially be recorded at their net proceeds, being the $100,000 raised less the $3,000 issue costs, giving $97,000. This should then be held at amortised cost, taking the effective rate of interest to the statement of profit or loss. The annual payment will be the coupon rate, which will be 5% × $100,000 = $5,000 a year.

Applying this to an amortised cost table gives $7,981, as shown below.

	B/f	Interest 8%	Payment	c/f
	$	$	$	$
20X4	97,000	7,760	(5,000)	99,760
20X5	99,760	**7,981**		

2 **A**

The default position for equity investments is fair value through profit or loss, meaning the investment is revalued each year end, with the gain or loss being taken to the statement of profit or loss.

3 **B**

Transaction costs are included when measuring all financial assets and liabilities at amortised costs, and when valuing financial assets valued at fair value through other comprehensive income.

Financial assets valued at fair value through profit or loss are expensed through the profit or loss account on initial valuation and not included in the initial value of the asset.

CHAPTER 11

1   D

Functional currency is defined as the currency of the primary economic environment in which an entity operates.

2   A

Overseas transactions are recorded in the functional currency using the spot rate of exchange. Therefore, the land is initially recorded at $10 million (30m dinars/3). Land is a non-monetary asset and so is not retranslated, meaning that its carrying amount remains as $10 million.

CHAPTER 12

1   C

Although the invoiced amount is $180,000, $30,000 of this has not yet been earned and must be deferred until the servicing work has been completed.

2   **0.16m**

Step 1 – Overall	$m
Price	5
Total cost – incurred to date	(1.6)
– estimated future	(2.4)
Overall profit	1

Step 2 – Progress

Progress = work certified 1.8/total price 5 = 36%

Step 3 – P/L	$m
Revenue (36% of 5)	1.8
Cost of sales (36% of 4m total costs)	(1.44)
Profit	0.36

Step 4 – SOFP	$m
Costs to date	1.6
Profit to date	0.36
Less: Amount billed	(1.8)
Contract asset	0.16

3   B

Whilst assessing the likelihood of economic benefits is part of identifying the contract, it is not listed as one of the five steps.

CHAPTER 13

1 D

The tax expense in the statement of profit or loss is made up of the current year estimate, the prior year overprovision and the movement in deferred tax. The prior year overprovision must be deducted from the current year expense, and the movement in deferred tax must be added to the current year expense, as the deferred tax liability has increased.

Tax expense = $60,000 – $4,500 + $600 = $56,100

2 C

Deferred tax provision required	9,000 (30,000 × 30%)
Opening balance per TB	12,000
Reduction in provision	(3,000)

Tax expense:

Current year estimate	15,000
Prior year overprovision	(4,000)
Deferred tax, as above	(3,000)
Charge for year	8,000

CHAPTER 14

1 D

(Basic) EPS for the year ended 30 September 20X7 ($15 million/43.25 million × 100)	$0.35	cents

Step 1 – Theoretical ex rights price (TERP)	
4 shares at $3.80	15.2
1 share at $2.80	2.8
5 shares at **$3.60** (TERP)	18

Step 2 – Rights fraction

Market value before issue/TERP = $3.80/$3.60

Step 3 – Weighted average number of shares

36 million × 3/12 × $3.80/$3.60	9.50	million
45 million × 9/12	33.75	million
	43.25	million

2   A

Diluted EPS for the year ended 30 September 2009		
($15.6 million/45.75 million × 100)	$0.34	
Adjusted earnings		
15 million + (10 million × 8% × 75%)	$15.6	million
Adjusted number of shares		
43.25 million + (10 million × 25/100)	45.75	million

3   C

(Basic) EPS for the year ended 30 September 20X7			
($12 million/43.2 million × 100)		$0.28	
Weighted average number of shares			
1 Oct	34 million × 4/12 × 6/5	13.6	million
1 Feb	37 million × 5/12 × 6/5	18.5	million
1 July	44.4 million × 3/12	11.1	million
		43.2	million

CHAPTER 15

1   A

(i)   Based upon the stated and publicised policy it would appear probable that customers who return goods in accordance with the policy will expect to receive a refund and so this requires a provision.

(ii)   The outcome of the legal claim has been assessed as only possible (rather than probable) that there will be an outflow of economic benefits. This does not require a provision, only a disclosure note of the contingent liability.

2   A

3   C

The warehouse fire is an adjusting event as it occurred before the reporting date. Settlement of the insurance claim should therefore be included in the financial statements.

The other events are non-adjusting as they occurred after the reporting date and do not provide evidence of conditions existing at the reporting date. Issue B is a brand new event, and therefore should not be adjusted. As it is clearly material, the event should be disclosed in the notes to the accounts.

CHAPTER 16

1   C

While having the majority of shares may be a situation which leads to control, it does not feature in the definition of control per IFRS 10.

2   C

The ability of one entity to exercise control over another is normally indicated by the ability to appoint the majority of the board of directors of that other entity. Significant influence over another is normally indicated by the ability to appoint at least one director to the board of that entity.

CHAPTER 17

1   C

	$
Reserves of Bina	400,000
Post-acquisition reserves of Maya – ($20,000 × 80%)	16,000
	416,000

2   B

	$
FV of NCI @ acquisition	25,000
Post-acquisition reserves of Calvin (15,000 – 10,000) × 40%	2,000
	27,000

3   Consolidated statement of financial position at 31 December 20X6

	$
Assets	
Non-current assets	
Property, plant & equip't ($300,000 + $225,000 + $30,000 FV adj)	555,000
Goodwill	230,000
Current assets	
Inventories ($80,000 + $75,000 – $5,000 PURP)	150,000
Trade and other receivables ($60,000 + $140,000)	200,000
Cash and cash equivalents ($10,000 + $25,000)	35,000
Total assets	1,170,000
Equity and liabilities	
Equity	
Share capital	80,000
Share premium	20,000
Retained earnings (W5)	370,000
Non-controlling interest (W4)	100,000
Total equity of the group	570,000
Non-current liabilities	
Loans ($300,000 + $85,000)	385,000
Current liabilities	
Trade and other payables ($155,000 + $60,000)	215,000
Total equity and liabilities	1,170,000

Refer to W3 for goodwill

Refer to W6 for PURP

Refer to W5 for retained earnings

Refer to W4 for NCI

Workings

(W1) Group structure

Picanto

80%

Sienna

(W2) Net assets of Sienna

	$	$	$
	Reporting date	Acquisition	Post –acq
Share capital	60,000	60,000	
Share premium	10,000	10,000	
Retained earnings	250,000	150,000	
FV uplift ($180,000 – $150,000)	30,000	30,000	
	350,000	250,000	100,000

(W3) Goodwill

	$
Consideration	400,000
Add: NCI at acquisition	80,000
Less net assets at acquisition (W2)	(250,000)
	230,000

(W4) Non-controlling interest

	$
NCI at acquisition	80,000
NCI % of Sienna post-acquisition retained earnings	20,000
(20% × $100,000 (W2))	
	100,000

(W5) Retained earnings

	$
100% of Picanto	295,000
PURP (W6)	(5,000)
80% of Sienna post-acquisition retained earnings	80,000
(80% × $100,000 (W2))	
	370,000

(W6) PURP

Profit = $50,000 × 25% = $12,500

Profit remaining in group inventory = $12,500 × 2/5 = $5,000

The correcting entry is:

Dr Retained earnings (W5) $5,000

Cr Inventories (SOFP) $5,000

CHAPTER 18

1   A

	$000
S2m + ($1.5m× 3/12) – $0.1m	2,275

2   B

	$000
NCI share of group profit after tax	
(400 × 6/12 × 40%)	80

Note: George made the intra-group sales and therefore bears all of the PURP adjustment. Only the post-acquisition element of Bungle's profit after tax is taken into account.

3   (a)   Goodwill on acquisition of Sultana

		$000
Fair value of consideration paid		25,000
FV of NCI at acquisition		7,000
Less: net assets of S at acquisition:		
Issued equity capital	4,000	
Retained earnings at acquisition	20,000	
		(24,000)
Goodwill on acquisition		8,000

(b)

> **KEY POINT** When dealing with a consolidated statement of profit or loss, always look to see whether the acquisition of the subsidiary was a mid-year acquisition during the year you are dealing with. If it was, remember to pro-rata each item of the subsidiary's income and expense so that your account only for the post-acquisition results in the group accounts.

Consolidated statement of profit or loss for the year ended 31 December 20X6

	$000
Revenue ($200,000 + (6/12 × $100,000) – $12,500 inter-co))	237,500
Cost of sales ($110,000 + (6/12 × $50,000) – $12,500 inter-co + $1,000 PURP)	(123,500)
Gross profit	114,000
Distribution costs ($20,000 + (6/12 × $10,000))	(25,000)
Administrative expenses ($40,000 + (6/12 × $20,000))	(50,000)
Profit before tax	39,000
Income tax expense ($10,500 + (6/12 × $6,000))	(13,500)
Profit after tax	25,500
Profit attributable to:	
Owners of Pecan (bal fig)	24,000
Non-controlling interest (W2)	1,500
	25,500

Refer to W1 for PURP

Refer to W2 for NCI

Workings

(W1) PURP and inter-company sales

Original cost plus 25% mark-up = $10m × 1.25 = $12,5m

This is the value of the inter-company sale and purchase which must be removed from both sales revenue and cost of sales.

Total profit on this sale = $12,5m – $10.0m = $2.5m

The proportion of this profit remaining in inventory must be eliminated:

40% × $2.5m = $1.0m

The double entry to adjust for this is:

Dr Cost of sales (P/L)　　　　$1m

Cr Inventory (SFP) $1m

(W2) Non-controlling interest

	$000
NCI % of (S's PAT – inter-co profit made by sub) (25% × ($7,000 – 1,000))	1,500

CHAPTER 19

1　(a)　Carrying amount of investment in Adil at 30 September 2009

	$000
Cost (40 million × 40% × $2)	32,000
Share of post-acquisition losses (5,000 × 40% × 6/12)	(1,000)
Impairment charge	(3,000)
Unrealised profit (6,000 × 20% × ½ × 40%)	(240)
	27,760

(b)　Petr Group

Consolidated statement of profit or loss for the year ended 30 September 2009

	$000	$000
Revenue (210,000 + (150,000 × 6/12) – 15,000 intra-group sales)		270,000
Cost of sales (W1)		(162,500)
Gross profit		107,500
Distribution costs (11,200 + (7,000 × 6/12))		(14,700)
Administrative expenses (18,300 + (9,000 × 6/12) + 2,000 impairment)		(24,800)
Investment income (W2)		1,100
Finance costs (W3)		(2,300)
Share of loss from associate (5,000 × 40% × 6/12)	(1,000)	
Impairment of investment in associate	(3,000)	
Unrealised profit in associate (see (a))	(240)	(4,240)
Profit before tax		62,560
Income tax expense (15,000 + (10,000 × 6/12))		(20,000)
Profit for the year		42,560

You can how the gure as one gure with a eparate orking or reak it down n the face f the CSPL.

Attributable to:

Owners of the parent	41,160
Non-controlling interest (W4)	1,400
	42,800

Workings (figures in brackets in $000)

(W1) Cost of sales

	$000
Petr	126,000
Simone (100,000 × 6/12)	50,000
Intra-group purchases	(15,000)
Additional depreciation: plant (5,000/5 years × 6/12)	500
Unrealised profit in inventories (15,000/3 × 20%)	1,000
	162,500

(W2) Investment income

	$000
Per statement of comprehensive income	9,500
Intra-group interest (50,000 × 8% × 6/12)	(2,000)
Intra-group dividend (8,000 × 80%)	(6,400)
	1,100

(W3) Finance costs

	$000
Petr	1,800
Simone post-acquisition ((3,000 – 2,000) × 6/12 + 2,000)	2,500
Intra-group interest (W2)	(2,000)
	2,300

CHAPTER 20

1

	True	False
If a subsidiary is disposed of on the last day of the reporting period then its assets and liabilities must still be included in the consolidated statement of financial position		X
The gain or loss arising on the disposal of a subsidiary in the financial statements is recorded in other comprehensive income		X

2   B

The profit or loss on the disposal is calculated as follows:

Proceeds	10m
Goodwill at disposal	(2m)
Net assets at disposal	(9m)
Non-controlling interest at disposal	3m
Profit on disposal	2m

3 $6,000,000

The profit arising in the individual financial statements of Hail will be the difference between the proceeds received of $10 million and the purchase price of $4 million.

CHAPTER 21

1   C

The current ratio is current assets divided by current liabilities: 5,800/2,200 = 2.64:1.

2   B

The quick ratio is: current assets less inventory divided by current liabilities, that is 2,000:2,200 = 0.9:1.

3   B

Prompt payment of suppliers' invoices will reduce the trade payables payment period. Buying proportionately more, or proportionately fewer, goods on credit will not affect calculation of the trade payables payment period. Offering a discount to credit customers will not affect the trade payables payment period.

4   C

An issue of ordinary shares will increase equity, and the repayment of a non-current liability loan will decrease +-liabilities. These two factors will combine to reduce the debt/equity ratio.

CHAPTER 22

1   A   False

    B   True

    C   True

    D   False

2   D

	$
Issue of shares (560,000 – 220,000)	340,000
Issue of loan notes	300,000
	640,000

Interest paid is included within the 'operating activities' heading of the cash flow statement.

3   C

	$
Profit	8,000
Add: depreciation (not a cash expense)	12,000
Less: purchase of new non-current assets	(25,000)
Fall in cash balance	(5,000)

4   D

Items added include the depreciation charge for the period, any losses on disposals of non-current assets, reductions in inventories and receivables (including prepayments) and any increase in trade payables (including accruals).

5

KEY POINT Ensure that you remember the proforma presentation of a statement of cash flows – it will help you to complete relevant extracts in an examination question.

Philomena – Statement of cash flows for the year ended 31 March 20X1

	$000	$000	Marks
Cash flows from operating activities			
Profit before tax	31,000		
Adjustments for:			
Depreciation charge	15,000		0.5
Loss on sale of plant and equipment	2,000		0.5
Interest payable	750		0.5
Increase in inventories ($36,000 – $30,000)	(6,000)		1.0
Increase in trade receivables ($40,000 – $35,000)	(5,000)		1.0
Increase in trade payables ($36,500 – $30,000)	6,500		1.0
	———		
Cash generated from operations	44,250		
Interest paid	(750)		0.5
Income taxes paid	(9,500)	34,000	1.0
	———		
Cash flows from investing activities			
Cash purchase of property, plant and equipment	(40,000)		1.0
Disposal proceeds of plant and equipment	8,000	(32,000)	1.0
	———		
Cash flows from financing activities			
Repayment of bank loan	(10,000)		1.0
Proceeds of share issue ($5,000 + $5,000)	10,000		2.0
Dividend paid	(14,000)	(14,000)	2.0
	———	———	
Increase in cash and cash equivalents ($10,000 + $2,000)		(12,000)	1.0
Cash and cash equivalents b/fwd		10,000	0.5
		———	
Cash and cash equivalents c/fwd (overdraft)		(2,000)	0.5
		———	———
			15.0

Refer to W3 for income taxes paid

Refer to W2 for disposal proceeds

Refer to W4 for bank loan

Refer to W6 for dividends paid

Refe W1 PPE

Refe W5 shar issue

Workings

(W1) PPE additions in the year

	$000
PPE CV bal b/fwd	93,000
Less: CV of disposals ($8,000 + $2,000 loss)	(10,000)
Less: depreciation charge	**(15,000)**
Revaluation in year	2,000
Cash paid for PPE additions	**40,000**
PPE CV bal c/fwd	110,000

(W2) Loss on disposal of plant and equipment

	$000
PPE CV of disposals ($8,000 + $2,000)	10,000
Less: loss on disposal in cost of sales	**(2,000)**
Disposal proceeds received	8,000

(W3) Income tax paid

	$000
Income tax liability b/fwd	10,000
Income tax charge for the year per P/L	6,000
Cash paid in year	**(9,500)**
Income tax liability c/fwd	6,500

(W4) Bank loan – amount repaid

	$000
Bank loan b/fwd	17,000
Cash paid	**(10,000)**
Bank loan c/fwd	7,000

(W5) Issue of shares in the year

	Share capital $000	Share premium $000
Balance b/fwd	15,000	3,000
Proceeds of share issue in year	**5,000**	**5,000**
Balance c/fwd	20,000	8,000

(W6) Dividend paid

	$000
Retained earnings b/fwd	85,000
Profit after tax for the year	25,000
Cash paid	**(14,000)**
Bank loan c/fwd	96,000

REFERENCES

The Board (2016) *Conceptual Framework for Financial Reporting*. London: IFRS Foundation.

The Board (2016) *IAS 1 Presentation of Financial Statements*. London: IFRS Foundation.

The Board (2016) *IAS 2 Inventories*. London: IFRS Foundation.

The Board (2016) *IAS 7 Statement of Cash Flows*. London: IFRS Foundation.

The Board (2016) *IAS 8 Accounting Policies, Changes in Accounting Estimates and Errors*. London: IFRS Foundation.

The Board (2016) *IAS 10 Events after the Reporting Period*. London: IFRS Foundation.

The Board (2016) *IAS 12 Income Taxes*. London: IFRS Foundation.

The Board (2016) *IAS 16 Property, Plant and Equipment*. London: IFRS Foundation.

The Board (2016) *IAS 20 Accounting for Government Grants and Disclosure of Government Assistance*. London: IFRS Foundation.

The Board (2016) *IAS 21 The Effects of Changes in Foreign Exchange Rates*. London: IFRS Foundation.

The Board (2016) *IAS 23 Borrowing Costs*. London: IFRS Foundation.

The Board (2016) *IAS 27 Separate Financial Statements*. London: IFRS Foundation.

The Board (2016) *IAS 28 Investments in Associates and Joint Ventures*. London: IFRS Foundation.

The Board (2016) *IAS 32 Financial Instruments*: Presentation. London: IFRS Foundation.

The Board (2016) *IAS 33 Earnings per Share*. London: IFRS Foundation.

The Board (2016) *IAS 36 Impairment of Assets*. London: IFRS Foundation.

The Board (2016) *IAS 37 Provisions, Contingent Liabilities and Contingent Assets*. London: IFRS Foundation.

The Board (2016) *IAS 38 Intangible Assets*. London: IFRS Foundation.

The Board (2016) *IAS 40 Investment Property*. London: IFRS Foundation.

The Board (2016) *IAS 41 Agriculture*. London: IFRS Foundation.

The Board (2016) *IFRS 3 Business Combinations*. London: IFRS Foundation.

The Board (2016) *IFRS 5 Non-current Assets Held for Sale and Discontinued Operations*. London: IFRS Foundation.

The Board (2016) *IFRS 7 Financial Instruments: Disclosure*. London: IFRS Foundation.

The Board (2016) *IFRS 9 Financial Instruments*. London: IFRS Foundation.

The Board (2016) *IFRS 10 Consolidated Financial Statements*. London: IFRS Foundation.

The Board (2016) *IFRS 13 Fair Value Measurement*. London: IFRS Foundation.

The Board (2016) *IFRS 15 Revenue from Contracts with Customers*. London: IFRS Foundation.

The Board (2016) *IFRS 16 Leases*. London: IFRS Foundation.

Index

Index

Index